NEXT GENERATION TALENT MANAGEMENT

NEXT GENERATION TALENT MANAGEMENT

Talent Management to Survive Turmoil

Andrés Hatum

Associate Professor, IAE Business School, Universidad Austral, Argentina
Director of CIGLA (Centro de Investigación "Guía Laboral")

First published 2010 by
PALGRAVE MACMILLAN

Palgrave Macmillan in the UK is an imprint of Macmillan Publishers Limited,
registered in England, company number 785998, of Houndmills, Basingstoke,
Hampshire RG21 6XS.

Palgrave Macmillan in the US is a division of St Martin's Press LLC,
175 Fifth Avenue, New York, NY 10010.

Palgrave Macmillan is the global academic imprint of the above companies
and has companies and representatives throughout the world.

Palgrave® and Macmillan® are registered trademarks in the United States,
the United Kingdom, Europe and other countries.

ISBN-13: 978–0–230–27929–2

This book is printed on paper suitable for recycling and made from fully
managed and sustained forest sources. Logging, pulping and manufacturing
processes are expected to conform to the environmental regulations of the
country of origin.

A catalogue record for this book is available from the British Library.

A catalog record for this book is available from the Library of Congress.

10   9   8   7   6   5   4   3   2   1
19 18 17 16 15 14 13 12 11 10

Printed and bound in Great Britain by
CPI Antony Rowe, Chippenham and Eastbourne

This book is dedicated to the memory of my mother, Hayat Hamade de Hatum (1949–2008)

CONTENTS

LIST OF TABLES AND FIGURES

Tables

Figures

ACKNOWLEDGMENTS

My principal objective when I started this book was to identify best practices in talent management worldwide to help managers build or improve their firms' talent management framework. The project took time to develop. Investigating state-of-the-art talent management strategies and practices required me to gain access to and visit many companies across the world to analyze the various practices in use, an endeavor that took over two years. Special thanks are due to those firms that made this book possible by providing me with an opportunity to understand their talent management models, strategies, and practices: L'Oréal; Syngenta; Dow; elBulli; Puig; Pfizer; Globant; Faena Hotel; Bimbo; Deloitte; Royal Mail; British American Tobacco; Aon; and lastminute.com.

Special thanks are also due to Guía Laboral, and company owner and friend Patricio Farcuh, who supported all the project's activities and trips, making quality research possible. To Professor Andrew Pettigrew, who helped me build my professional identity towards an academic life. His insight, generosity, and friendship deserve my lifelong gratitude. To Ethna Pettigrew and Brenda Priebke, who helped me enhance various drafts of this project and also supported me in thinking over some ideas of the book.

My thanks extend to my friends, who are always close to me whenever needed and encouraged me to finish this work. Adriana Urquía; Santiago G. Belmonte; Javier Quintanilla, Mariana and Mariano Tasín; Lorenzo Preve; and Ezequiel Garbers deserve my recognition and love. To my parents, who taught me the meaning of both hard work and happiness. My father always insisted on the value of learning and being a leader in one's field. My mother showed me the importance of working to achieve one's aims. Both granted me the gift and opportunity to study whatever I wanted, and only now do I realize the significance of such an opportunity. Finally, thanks to my family, Gabriela, Nicolás, Sofía, and Victoria. Their support and love made this work possible. To them I dedicate this book.

FOREWORD

This is a sound and accessible book on one of the key management topics of the day. It will be of great practical value to reflective senior managers and human resource (HR) specialists contemplating the issue of how to attract, develop, and retain talented and motivated employees.

We are regularly told of the ever-changing nature of work, and the scarcity of talent and the productivity of people in the world. The nature of jobs is changing – where we work, how we work, and what we think of work may all be in transition. Globalizing firms are faced with constant pressures to find the best talent they can as the supply and demand for people wavers in different economies and sectors over time. There is plenty of evidence to show that the scarcity of talent has placed constraints on the growth patterns of firms and that even the most sophisticated organizations seem only to become aware of these talent scarcities after they have made big strategic business moves. The anticipation and proactive management of employment issues are apparently rare phenomena and are deserving of research in their own right.

But today's talent issues are not just about shortages and constraints on growth and development. The economic downturn experienced since 2008 and continuing into 2010 is affecting organizations worldwide. Many organizations are managing down costs and the effects are particularly visible in low-end services and manufacturing. There has also been further pressure to save money by off-shoring. Critical talent shortages may still exist in certain sectors, but the developmental agenda which often exposes talent shortages is happening at the same time as firms are seeking to make efficiencies in the employment of people.

Tackling current talent management challenges requires a reflective, anticipatory, and integrative point of view. This means thinking across business, economic, and demographic changes as well as organizational, behavioral, and attitudinal factors inside the firm. And as Andrés Hatum argues, it is also dependent on co-ordinative and sensitive awareness and action involving both senior managers and senior human resource specialists.

This book by Andrés Hatum meets many of the analytical and practical challenges posed by the above agenda. Hatum places talent management firmly in a business, economic, and organizational context. The book is aware of the sensitive political and co-ordinative relations between line managers and human resource specialists, and an integrative point of view is offered linking macro-environmental changes to demographic changes and the dynamics of new forms of organizing.

The conceptual frameworks in the book offer illuminating maps to aid the thinking of the reflective practitioner and the book as a whole is organized around the core themes and challenges of how to attract talent, how to develop talent, and how to retain talent.

The analysis in the book is brought to life by a series of meaningful case studies drawn from well-known companies in North America, Latin America, and Europe. The summaries offered at the end of each chapter highlight managerial consequences and list a series of 'very important questions'. These questions will be of particular value to the practicing manager. Posing and illustrating pertinent questions is often much more valuable to the reflective practitioner than offering simple answers.

Professor Andrew M. Pettigrew
Saïd Business School
University of Oxford, 2010

1

INTRODUCTION

Talent is a gift that must be cultivated, not left to languish
Ed Michaels, Helen Handfield-Jones,
and Beth Axelrod

There was a time when organizations and organizational theorists could easily explain what was expected of employees: organizations were hierarchical systems or mechanisms (Hatch, 1997) in which status was both important and a symbol of recognition. Employees respected this hierarchy. Homogeneity and stability in the workplace were paramount and job stability shaped organizational life.

The equilibrium firms achieved during that era provided employers and employees with clear benefits and responsibilities. Employers needed to guarantee stable jobs and, in many cases, jobs for life; while this might be unrealistic today, it was feasible in the era of organizational stability. In turn, employees were expected to be loyal towards the organization and recognize the firm's hierarchy. Most employees were happy with this fairy-tale arrangement. They got jobs. They could expect to retire from the company they first started to work with. They respected their bosses. Any position they achieved would have been earned.

Fairy tales do not last long, however. The context within which firms were operating (the outer context) became both more competitive and more complex. Firms' inner context then followed suit. Organizations needed to adapt quickly to the changes posed by the business environment and they also needed to transform radically. Thus, the era of stability was replaced by an era of rapid changes and turbulence. Moreover, the old homogeneous workforce became a heterogeneous one in which, as Gladwell (2008) points out, various generations worked and

1

overlapped. Talent issues not considered previously now demanded attention.

These changes, which will be explained throughout this book, transformed the importance of talent management. Before, talent could be considered largely part of human resource's domain. Now, in an era characterized by workforce heterogeneity and fast-changing, fast-paced environments, talent has become an organizational issue of concern to top management, line managers, and human resources alike. Everybody is, or should be, involved in managing talent.

This book aims to help top managers, line managers, and HR generalists and specialists understand the organizational transformations that have occurred and thus, the new talent challenges they have to confront. It also aims to offer something that is possibly more important for practitioners, namely, strategies and tools that can be put into action to tackle the new talent challenges. Discussion of such strategies and tools is accompanied by case studies of real companies and examples to provide concrete insight into the world of talent.

As already suggested, this book may be read by top managers, line managers, and HR managers and specialists. The theoretical insights, plus the practical tools and real-world examples, will help people in these roles to plan and think proactively about talent management. However, the book may also be useful for students of MBA and Executive MBA programs and for students of management in its diverse specializations. For them, the book can be a guide of best practices on the one hand, and a resource that gives some conceptual understanding on the other.

The book is organized into chapters that attempt to explain the macro and micro context of talent management. This introductory chapter aims to further understanding of the macro influences that have shaped organizations' talent management. Chapter 2 sheds light on various concepts such as talent management, individual and organizational talent, and the scope of talent. Roles and responsibilities in the talent management process are also analyzed.

Chapters 3, 4, and 5 turn to the talent management model that is, attracting, developing, and retaining employees. These chapters are useful for practitioners, as they offer models and clear examples of the different dimensions of talent management being analyzed. In Chapter 3, for example, the different aspects of the attraction process, such as the employee value proposition (EVP), recruitment, and selection, are analyzed. In Chapter 4, themes such as talent pools, succession planning, identification of talent from within, performance, competencies, and potential are considered. Chapter 5 takes up the challenge of analyzing a long-term retention model and explores organizational identity, compensation, rewards, careers, and employability. Finally, chapter 6 attempts to link the three main dimensions of our talent management model, namely, attraction, development, and retention.

The book, in addition to providing various examples that help illustrate a particular strategy or practice, also highlights 'best practices at a glance' – these are state-of-the-art talent management practices used by leading companies around the world. Four 'cases in point' are included to provide even deeper understanding of a particular company's strategy and actions. Table 1.1 summarizes the best practices that will be highlighted in this book. Table 1.2 reviews the cases in point that will be analyzed.

TABLE 1.1 **Best practices highlighted in this book**

Company name	Best practice analyzed	Industry	Country
Southwest Airlines	Employee value proposition (EVP)	Aviation/ transportation	USA
Cirque du Soleil	Recruiting	Entertainment	Canada
Red 5 Studios	Recruitment channels	Video games	USA
Faena Hotel + Universe	Selection	Hotel	Argentina
Puig	Talent pools	Fragrance, cosmetics, and fashion	Spain
Pfizer	Development and performance	Pharmaceutical	USA
Deloitte	Learning and development	Consulting/auditing	USA
Globant	Career development	IT outsourcing	Argentina
Bimbo	Organizational identity	Food/baking	Mexico

TABLE 1.2 **Cases in point analyzed**

Company name	Strategy analyzed	Industry	Country
elBulli	Individual and organizational talent	Gastronomy	Spain
L'Oréal	Attraction	Beauty	France
Syngenta	Development and learning	Agribusiness	Switzerland
Dow	Retention	Chemical	USA

1.1 WHY AND HOW HAVE WE ARRIVED AT THIS SITUATION?

Dealing with talent always has been, and always will be, challenging. Why is it that, these days, every organization is so concerned (even desperate) about this issue? There have always been talented people. But over time, talent management has become less of a simple managerial matter dealt with by a department, and more of a huge problem with an enormous impact on the future of the firm's sustainability. The 1950s are often looked back upon as the era of 'lifetime employment' (Capelli, 2008a) in which people were proud and happy to be a part of a company. This era was also characterized by business stability and growth. At that time, it was frequent to find a job and stay there for as long as your professional career lasted. Job-hopping was not considered something to be proud of; indeed, it was judged to be a marker of career failure. Consequently, firms had to develop talent within the firm, as it was very difficult to hire qualified personnel from outside the firm.

But the context has changed and with it the role of talent in organizations. Since the 1990s a new business context has emerged, characterized by macro-environmental changes, changes in the way firms are organized (Hatum, 2007), and demographic transformation. The macro-environmental changes affecting businesses have been shaped by an acceleration in the rate of change in the economic, social, technological, and political worlds. March (1995) underlines four factors that have increased the degree of volatility and uncertainty in the environment in which firms operate: global linkages, that is, the business networks that cause global interdependencies to multiply and national boundaries to fade; information technology, which enhances the possibilities for co-ordinating and controlling organizations; knowledge-based competition, that is, the use of knowledge as a primary source of competitive advantage; and political uncertainty, that is, the loss of autonomy of the national state through a general loss of control of boundaries. All these factors have caused competition to intensify, product lifecycles to shorten, and technological innovation to increase – in short, these factors have led to hypercompetition. In this context, D'Aveni (1994) indicates that the choice is clear for managers: either stand still and resist the environmental changes, or actively adapt to the environment and take advantage of its opportunities. D'Aveni (1994, p. 356) notes that in a dynamic world, only dynamic firms that can adapt rapidly to hypercompetitive environments will survive.

The increase in volatility and uncertainty is shaping the world in which we live. Indeed, the financial and economic crisis of 2008/09, which has led to worldwide market declines of a scale not seen since the 1930s, may have yet-to-be-revealed consequences for the way we work, organize, and compete (Beechler & Woodward, 2009). In turn, talent management will surely be shaped by the way companies ultimately deal with the current crisis.

Over the last decade, management literature has called for new forms of organizing to confront uncertain and hypercompetitive environments. Theories on ideal types of organization have, therefore, proliferated in an attempt to identify ways for firms to adapt rapidly under high levels of competition. Organizational designs that have been suggested take names such as the agile and virtual enterprise (Goranson, 1999); the N-form (Hedlund, 1994); the innovative firm (Pettigrew & Fenton, 2000); the adaptive firm (Haeckel, 1999); the agile firm (Goldman et al., 1995); the chaordic enterprise (van Eijnatten & Putnik, 2004); and the flexible firm (Volberda, 1999; Hatum & Pettigrew, 2006; Hatum, 2007).

Rather than focus on ideal ways of organizing, however, Pettigrew & Fenton (2000) and Pettigrew et al. (2003) attempt to understand the ways in which firms actually organize themselves to adapt to competitive contexts. In the conclusion of their European survey, Pettigrew and his colleagues find that the most adaptable and innovative firms have combined changes in structure (e.g., more decentralization, delayering and project forms of organization), changes in processes (e.g., more horizontal communication, investments in information technology, and innovations in human resource practices), and changes in boundaries (e.g., more downscoping, outsourcing, and strategic alliances).

In addition to the above factors, demographic changes have also led to the talent challenges companies face today. Baby Boomers are heading towards retirement, Generation X (Gen X) is exhausted, and Generation Y (Gen Y), or the Millennial generation as it is also called, doesn't seem to care about the values of previous generations.[1] Before the 1980s, employees valued stability. The great downsizing and corporate transformation of the 1980s, however, destroyed employee loyalty to companies. Thus, when the dot.com boom of the 1990s produced a surge of job opportunities, job-hopping became an important part of a person's career – no longer a sign of failure, as in the era of lifetime employment (Capelli, 2008a). Twenty years ago, for example, those individuals leaving UK schools and universities could expect to experience a maximum of two different jobs by the age of 25. In 2006, in contrast, this figure had increased to four jobs.[2]

While Baby Boomers and Gen X have acknowledged this transition, the contrary can be said about Gen Y, who have quite different

TABLE 1.3 **Generations over time: main characteristics**

Generation	Main events	Characteristics
Baby boomers	Witnesses of the cold war	Patient
	Civil rights struggle	Committed
		Loyal
Generation X	Technological development	Empowered
		Optimistic
	Fall of the Berlin Wall	Practical/pragmatic
		Adaptable/responsive to change
		Self-reliant
		Individualistic
Generation Y	Witnesses of the war on terrorism	Ambitious
		Creative
	Technological boom	Emphasize work–life balance
		Informal
		Technologically savvy
		Teamworking
		Multitasking

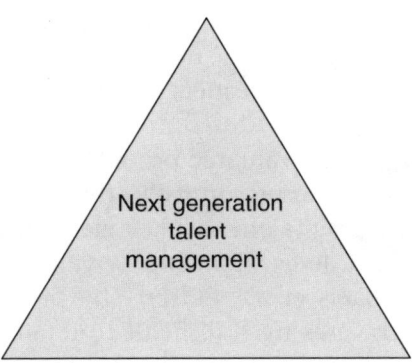

FIGURE 1.1 **Next generation talent management: influential issues**

values compared with their parents. Previous generations were raised with principles such as commitment to the company, promotion from within, and the idea of a job for life. In contrast, Gen Y aims for self-gratification and instant enjoyment, along with the spoils that come with it, not wanting to suffer as their parents did. Table 1.3 summarizes the main features and events that shaped each generation.

The confluence of the macro-environmental changes, the new ways of organizing, and the demographic changes of recent years has led to what is referred to in this book as 'next generation talent management', as captured by Figure 1.1.

1.2 TIME OF REVENGE: EMPLOYEES' GOLDEN ERA

After years of an ever-changing context, which this book has already described, companies started implementing a number of procedures aimed to ensure their survival over time. In particular, delayering, outsourcing, rightsizing, and downscoping were the 'solutions' that organizations employed to stop the bleeding (at least that was what they believed). The results of these procedures were flatter structures, new forms of organizing, and a large quantity of consultants, who flocked into companies with grand ideas that made employees tremble with fear – everything ending with -*ing* was synonymous with disaster for many people who lost their jobs. Today, skilled employees are becoming a scarce resource for many organizations. Because of this, companies are investing in recruiting, searching for the best talent they can find in today's slim market. As a recent Global Talent Index highlighted,[3] China and India are the new rising stars in the global talent war. And as these new global leaders are emerging, a talent void is beginning to appear.

Formerly, when companies evaluated production locations, not only were costs considered but also proximity to different markets. Today, companies are also regarding talent as a key element in their location decisions.[4] There is a great demand for highly valued and high-calibre managerial talent (Michaels et al., 2001). The best people are constantly offered new jobs, making it difficult to retain them over long periods of time. Talented people know they are at an advantage when it comes to negotiation, in contrast to the suffering they were put through in the 1980s. This is the game firms are obliged to play today; a game of stakes, which affects companies' operations and, in turn, can negatively affect firms' bottom lines if they do not anticipate their future talent needs and have a clear talent strategy to meet their anticipated needs.

Table 1.4 points out the main transformations the business and talent realities have been through. The previous stability is now characterized by complexity, which includes crises and market jolts. The long-term career path has been replaced by people changing jobs frequently to mould their careers according to their wishes. Not surprisingly, therefore, an increase in hiring from outside the firm has replaced the old paradigm of raising people from within only. The increase in labor market mobility has decreased the commitment of employees to the

TABLE 1.4 **Business and talent realities: trends over time**

Business and talent stability	Next generation talent management
Business stability	Business complexity
Raising people from within	Searching for outside talent
Career development in a few companies	Job-hopping
Commitment to the organization	Self-commitment
Negotiation power: the company	Negotiation power: the person
Job security: critical	Job security: an old-fashioned value

organization, with a shift in commitment towards self-commitment. Moreover, today's employees do not value job security as they did before; rather, they feel powerful because they are aware of their importance to organizations.

In this context, companies need to have a clear model of talent management, and this model needs to be shared throughout the organization. This is an important step towards facing the challenges of rapid business and talent changes in an era of talent shortages.

CHAPTER HIGHLIGHTS

❖ Three main changes have influenced talent in recent decades:

- *Macro-environmental changes*, such as globalization, information technology, knowledge-based competition and political, economic, and financial uncertainty.
- *New forms of organizing*, which have shifted the traditional hierarchical structure towards leaner and flatter organization.
- *Demographic changes*, which require that companies learn how to deal with three overlapping generations: Baby Boomers, Gen Xers and Gen Yers.

❖ The main consequences of the foregoing issues are:

- Lifetime employment is over.
- Job-hopping is the new trend among the younger generation of workers.
- Talent management is now of strategic importance for the whole organization.

VERY IMPORTANT QUESTIONS

- What is the nature of talent management in the context within which the organization is working?
- What are the key strategic challenges that the organization faces in its approach to talent management?
- Does the global labor market affect the firm?
- Does a diverse workforce in terms of generational differences influence the firm's talent management?

2

TALENT MANAGEMENT

Talent, top talent, critical talent, and talent management – these are all related to the topic in question. But therein lies a problem in discussing talent: it seems that everyone has their own idea of what the word *talent* describes or captures. Broadly speaking, talent refers to the skills or capabilities that allow a person to perform a certain task. Michaels et al. (2001, p. xii) define talent as 'the sum of a person's abilities – his or her intrinsic gifts, skills, knowledge, experience, intelligence, judgment, attitude, character, and drive. It also includes his or her ability to learn and grow.'

A good definition of talent management, however, is more difficult to pin down. As Lewis & Heckman (2006) point out, it is very difficult to identify a precise meaning of talent management because of both confusion regarding definitions of terms used and differences in assumptions made by authors who write about the issue. For instance, Lewis & Heckman note that the terms talent strategy, succession management, and human resource planning are often used interchangeably. Further, in a 2006 learning and development survey,[1] only 20% of respondents specifically noted that they had a formal definition of talent management and, although 51% of respondents claimed that their organizations undertook talent management activities, a general lack of consistency can be seen in the respondents' definitions of talent management. Thus, before presenting a definition of talent management, it is necessary to first develop an understanding of what talent management encompasses by discussing some of the attributes commonly used to characterize it. Table 2.1 provides a summary of these attributes.

Based upon the attributes presented in Table 2.1, it is possible to distinguish several approaches to talent management. One approach relates talent management to traditional HR practices such as recruitment, selection, training, and performance measurement, among

TABLE 2.1 Attributes commonly used to characterize talent management

Author / Focus of analysis	Attraction	Development	Retention	Human capital/strategy	Strategic approach	Talent pool	Talent mindset	Employee value proposition	Recruitment/selection	Training	Performance	Potential	Leadership	People/individual talent	Personal capital	Career development/path	Processes	Succession	Employee education	Organizational development	Talent model	Diversity	Technology	Scanning the environment
Branham, 2001		X																						
Cohen, 2001									X															
Michaels et al., 2001	X	X	X		X	X	X	X																
Robertson & Abbey, 2003								X	X		X			X										
Sears, 2003					X																			X
Rothwell & Kazanas, 2004		X			X					X									X	X				X
Brown & Hesketh, 2004				X											X				X	X				
Kermally, 2004		X			X																			
Schweyer, 2004																							X	
Barner, 2006													X											
Rueff & Stringer, 2006	X	X	X									X				X	X	X						
Smilansky, 2006		X														X	X	X				X		

11

TABLE 2.1 (Continued)

Author	Attraction	Development	Retention	Human capital/strategy	Strategic approach	Talent pool	Talent mindset	Employee value proposition	Recruitment/selection	Training	Performance	Potential	Leadership	People/individual talent	Personal capital	Career development/path	Processes	Succession	Employee education	Organizational development	Talent model	Diversity	Technology	Scanning the environment
Davis et al., 2007		X	X						X															
Thorne & Pellant, 2007			X			X			X	X														
Berke et al., 2008		X	X										X											
Capelli, 2008b					X																X			
Cheese et al., 2008				X							X													
Colvin, 2008														X										
Fulmer & Bleak, 2008		X																						
Lawler III, 2008				X																				
Coyle, 2009														X										
Schiemann, 2009					X						X										X			

12

other things (Cohen, 2001; Robertson & Abbey, 2003; Cheese et al., 2008). This approach is not new; rather, the traditional HR practices are becoming more critical to a firm's success and thus, it is becoming more important to link these practices to the talents required by firms.

A different approach towards talent management is closely related to the idea of HR planning, strategic HR management, and succession planning (Rothwell & Kazanas, 2004). Rothwell & Kazanas, for instance, outline the strategic importance of talent management, while others highlight the importance of talent pools for succession purposes. However, this stream of the literature fails to 'advance the theory or practice of HR' (Lewis & Heckman, 2006, p. 141).

A third approach towards talent management takes a more general view, linking talent management to issues such as leadership (Barner, 2006), talent pools (Michaels et al., 2001), an individual's potential (Smilansky, 2006), the development of talent (Fulmer & Bleak, 2008), and the attraction and retention of personnel (Rueff & Stringer, 2006).

Unfortunately, the three approaches to talent management mentioned above fail to fully clarify the concept of talent management itself. Neither of the first two approaches described explains the concept of talent management nor sheds light on how to manage talent through a better understanding of HR planning or practices. The third approach isn't particularly convincing due to its lack of focus and depth with respect to topics covered. In addition, none of the three approaches is strategic or tied to a firm's underlying business strategy, and hence the three approaches necessarily limit the potential impact of talent management. Indeed, following the previous approaches, talent management would simply be another aspect of the HR area. Later in this book it will become clear that the scope of talent management extends well beyond the HR department alone.

Based upon Table 2.1 and discussion, it is now possible to present a definition of talent management. For the purpose of this book, talent management is *a strategic activity aligned with the firm's business strategy that aims to attract, develop, and retain talented employees at each level of the organization*. The talent-planning process, therefore, is linked directly to a firm's business and strategic-planning processes.

At the core of this definition is the employee. Consistent with Barney (1991, 1995), Vance & Vaiman (2008), and Lewis & Heckman (2006), talent management is rooted in the resource-based theory of organizations, which states that sustained competitive advantage is only possible for firms that develop resources that are valuable, rare, and hard to imitate. Talent management focuses on how an organization can generate and maintain such resources through its human capital. In doing so, talent management has come to focus on talent at the organizational level rather than at the individual employee level. Put differently, rather than ask how an individual's talent can support the firm, talent management asks how an organization's talent structure can be fine-tuned by attracting, developing, and retaining people. By being a leader in such activities, a firm can develop organizational capabilities that are valuable, rare, and hard to imitate, and hence can enjoy a sustained competitive advantage.

In the discussion above, a distinction is made between talent at the individual level and talent management at the organizational level. Figure 2.1 sheds more light on the difference between (individual) talent and (organizational) talent management. As Figure 2.1 shows, by concentrating on talent at the individual level, a firm can attract 'A' players (or stars) who will shine within the firm, but who may not necessarily contribute to the firm's ability to compete and succeed. In contrast, by taking an organizational view of talent management, firms can consider talent in a more holistic way, linking individuals' talent with their organizational life and thereby developing the organization's comparative advantage.

Note that, as Figure 2.1 shows, the talent management perspective is based in part on the idea that talent can be found at all

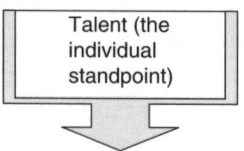

- Considers 'A' players, or individuals with high skill, the subjects of interest
- May create 'lone rangers'

- Talent can be found at all levels of the organization
- Links talent with the individual's organizational life
- Treats talent as an organizational capability
- Develops talent as a competitive advantage, making it 'rare, valuable, and difficult to imitate'

FIGURE 2.1 **Individual and organizational talent**

levels of an organization. This view captures the fact that all levels of an organization contribute to the firm's performance, and is also consistent with Guthridge et al. (2008), who suggest that talent management should be targeted at all levels of the organization. Accordingly, in this book talent refers not only to an organization's 'A' players, but also to employees who are not necessarily being developed to eventually become part of the company's top team. Focusing only on 'A' players 'can damage the morale of the rest of the organization and, as a result, overall performance' (Guthridge et al., 2008, p. 56). Similarly, talent management is taken to focus not on the top team only, but on the organization as a whole. In summary, this book gives a balanced consideration to those processes and activities that attract, develop, and retain talent at all layers of the organization.

In practice, the top team ('A' players in Michaels et al., 2001) or an elite subgroup of future leaders of the organization are often the focus of talent strategies. In a survey conducted by the Chartered Institute of Personnel and Development (CIPD),[2] for example, 40% of respondents indicate that the main targets of their talent management programs are their high-potential employees, while slightly fewer organizations report including managerial-level employees in their talent management activities.

Following our perspective, however, other 'players' are critical as well when planning a talent management strategy. For example, *managers* and *middle managers* are essential to making sure the business' operation is successful, and *high potentials* are necessary to provide a pool of future managers or key actors within the organization. *Critical talent*, which may be found at all levels within the firm, can also become key contributors to a company's strategy. Thus, key positions are not necessarily restricted to the top team, but are likely to include positions at lower levels as well. Figure 2.2 summarizes some of the key types of players that are important to include in a comprehensive talent management strategy.

The above discussion implies that an organizational-level talent management perspective requires a high level of maturity, where talent management is not only aligned with the firm's strategy, but also informs corporate strategy. From this standpoint, it is important to work with a wide scope of talents within an organization. It is important to note, however, that there is no single blueprint for effective talent management. Different organizations have different levels of

FIGURE 2.2 **Scope of talent management within the organization**

FIGURE 2.3 **Talent management: strategy and scope**

sophistication, different concerns, and different requirements. This makes a single model difficult to apply to all organizational contexts. The variation across organizations' maturity in the area of talent management is depicted in Figure 2.3.

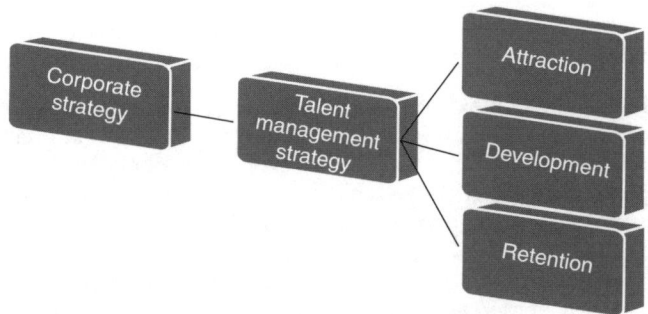

FIGURE 2.4 **Talent, strategy and the organization**

The maturity of a firm's talent management program will determine whether the scope of talent management focuses on individual-level talent or the organization. To be able to broaden the scope of talent, organizations need to make sure that they deploy a talent management strategy in which issues such as talent attraction, development, and retention are viewed as critical strategic factors for the success of the firm's overall business strategy. Without such a strategic view in which talent informs, and is informed by, the firm's overall strategy, any talent management implementation may fail. Figure 2.4 shows the links between business and talent management strategy.

So, the aim of talent management is to link an organization's enterprise-wide talent to the firm's strategy. But who is responsible for talent management within the organization? This question is addressed in the following section.

Off the record

Talent and organizational schizophrenia

'Talent is our most critical asset.' Many employers repeat variations of this statement over and over again. Yet if one considers the situation of most companies today, it is clear that often such claims amount more to wishful thinking than a reflection of a company's true conditions. Which begs the question: is talent a critical asset?

If talent is indeed regarded as a critical asset and a source of competitive advantage, companies need to avoid organizational schizophrenia. In schizophrenic organizations, top management tends to say one thing but

(Continued)

do another. In the context of talent, schizophrenic organizations emphasize the importance of talent and the significance of people, but in practice may not pay market salaries and may not invest in developing their employees, etc. Employees facing such a scenario come to distrust the organization. In turn, any talent management strategy in place is disregarded and ultimately ditched for lack of support. Thus, if a company truly regards talent as an important organizational asset, it must take care to be coherent and consistent in the implementation of its talent management strategy.

2.1 THE MANAGEMENT OF TALENT

To put a talent management strategy into practice, an organization first has to address the question of who will be in charge of this process. Common sense might suggest that the HR department should lead the process. However, common sense is not always the best evaluator or guide. Indeed, if you want the process to fail from the start, asking the HR department to own it and champion it would be a good way to proceed. The reason is that implementation of the firm's talent management strategy should be conducted at every level of the organization, and thus the firm's top management should lead the way for the rest to follow. The HR department must, of course, have an important role in this process, but only after the CEO and other top managers have regarded it as a strategic matter that is a central part of their agenda. Note that the HR department's value and expertise is not being underestimated here; human resources can be of a great relevance when implementing and executing the talent management process. However, because the difficulties that a talent management process may face do not stem from the HR office only, but from the degree of commitment from and collaboration among the CEO, top managers, and line managers (Guthridge et al., 2008), an organization-wide 'talent mindset' (Michaels et al., 2001; Cheese et al., 2008) that starts at the top is key to the successful implementation of a talent management strategy.

Because a talent mindset requires the engagement of the entire organization, starting from the top, it is imperative that the CEO and top management team have a talent agenda. A talent agenda makes talent issues part of top management's daily responsibilities. Further, a talent agenda helps make top management accountable for establishing talent standards for the organization. This is important because it helps leaders recognize that talent management requires investment of real money and that talent reviews are strategic issues.

A recent study conducted by the Economist Intelligence Unit (2006) found that, indeed, CEOs tend to be highly involved in the talent management process. Respondent CEOs argued that talent management is too critical for their firms to be left to human resources alone. This is not surprising given the increased importance of talent management to a firm's overall success. For instance, in a recent analysis that covered academic and practitioner journals since 2004, Mascarenhas (2009) concludes that in the emerging CEO agenda, competing for talent is one of the seven issues a CEO must consider critical for the success of the firm's strategy and, in turn, for his or her own job.

There is another reason why a firm's talent management strategy should be led by top management. Say that line managers were instead the owners of a firm's talent management initiatives. Now consider the impact of line managers who are not committed to the talent management process. Rather than facilitate the development or performance of their employees, such managers are likely to present obstacles to productive employees trying to access organizational opportunities. Thus, as Heinen & O'Neill (2004) point out, CEOs should be the ultimate owners of the talent management process.

What role, then, should the HR department play in a new organizational architecture based on talent management? Human resources is an enabler, a catalyst; the area most involved in strategic talent decisions. Talent management thus provides a great opportunity to show the strategic importance of the the HR department. Figure 2.5 summarizes the different roles and responsibilities of top managers (including CEOs), line managers, and HR managers in the talent management process.

In practice, however, HR departments rarely take advantage of this opportunity. Keith Hammonds' (2005, p. 40) critical article on the HR area illustrates the crisis the area has gone through over the years: 'After close to 20 years of hopeful rhetoric about becoming "strategic partners" with a "seat at the table" where the business decisions that matter are made, most human-resources professionals aren't nearly there. They have no seat, and the table is locked inside a conference room to which they have no key. HR people are, for most practical purposes, neither strategic nor leaders.' More recently, Lawler III (2008, p. 152)

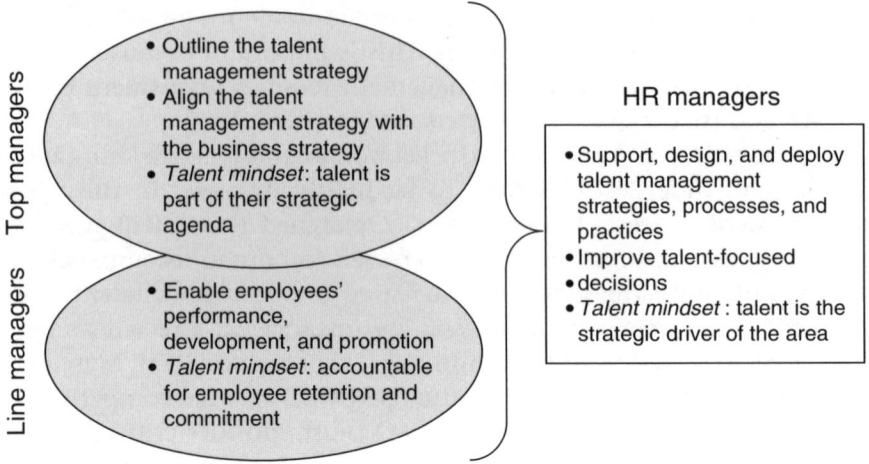

FIGURE 2.5 **Roles and responsibilities in talent management**

asserts that 'HR is not and never has been a major player when it comes to talent management and organizational effectiveness'.

Figure 2.6 shows the evolutionary pattern of the HR area within organizations. The evolution path proceeds from the personnel

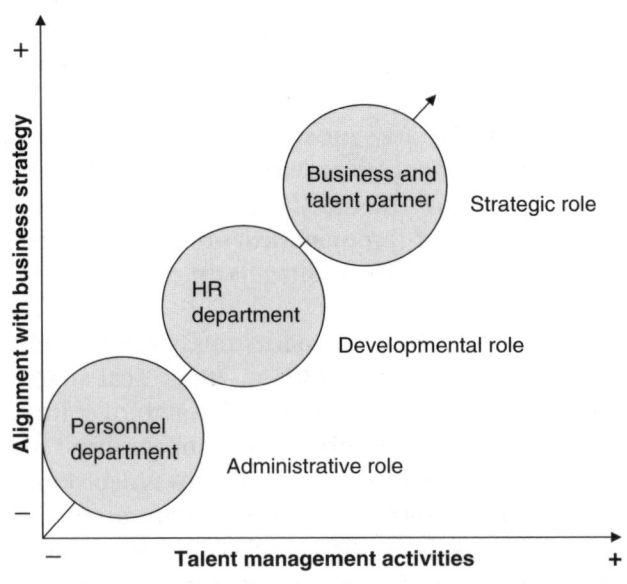

FIGURE 2.6 **HR evolutionary pattern**

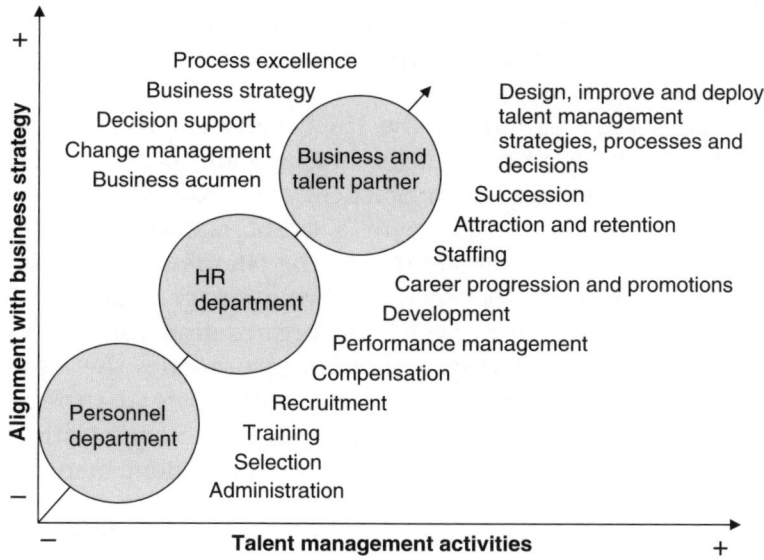

FIGURE 2.7 **HR practices and processes needed to become a business and talent partner**

department, to the HR department, to what we call a *business and talent partner*. The more the HR department is aligned with the company's business strategy, and the more talent management activities it accounts for, the closer the HR professional is to becoming a business and talent partner.

However, following this evolutionary path is not so easy. Figure 2.7, which builds on Figure 2.6, stresses the practices and processes that an HR area needs to excel at to become a business and talent partner.

The above discussion may paint a rather bleak picture of the ability of an organization's HR area to actually play a strategic role in talent management. However, as suggested earlier, while human resources may have lost its flair and maybe its strategic place and status, the fact that talent management is a strategic activity offers the HR area an opportunity to elevate its status in the organization. To take advantage of this opportunity, HR personnel should develop the area's ability to assist in the design and implementation of talent management strategies. Indeed, Boudreau & Ramstad (2005, pp. 20–1) suggests that enhancing the strategic role of human resources requires that human resources be equipped 'to improve talent decisions throughout the organization', and more importantly, that human resources has a 'talent-focused perspective for improving decisions, not just a process for implementing decisions'.

The evolutionary pattern of the HR department thus consists of developing an ability to excel at the practices and processes depicted in Figure 2.7. Developing such practices and processes increases an organization's ability to implement a talent management strategy, and thus increases the strategic role of the HR area. Figure 2.8 summarizes the relationship between the evolutionary stage of a firm's HR area and the degree to which an organization can implement a talent management strategy. Figure 2.8 incorporates the ideas presented in previous figures in this chapter and shows that the role of the HR department in terms of its maturity in the organization limits the extent to which firms can undertake any talent management activity.

As Figure 2.8 illustrates, those firms in which the HR area serves simply as a personnel department will find it difficult to create any

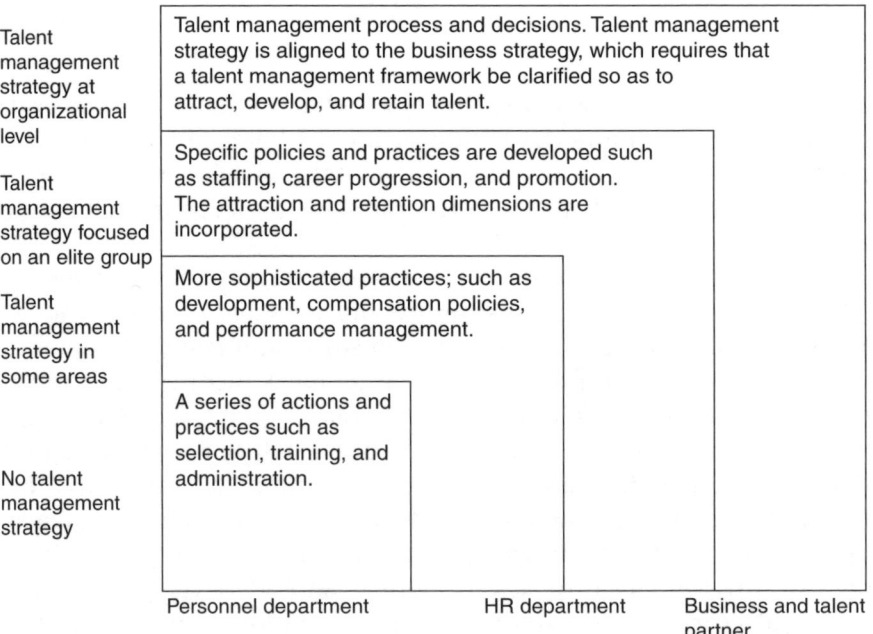

FIGURE 2.8 **Talent management scope and HR stages**

process, activity or culture of talent management. An HR department, in contrast, may be able to design talent management strategies and activities for some areas or for an elite group of management, while a business and talent partner, that is, an HR department able to align the firm's talent management strategy with the firm's overall strategy, will be able to design, develop, and deploy a talent management strategy at the organizational level.

One of the questions that organizations need to answer when designing their talent management strategy is: what roles need to be involved in the talent management process? As discussed above, the involvement of line managers in addition to the CEO and the top management team will increase the success of the firm's talent management strategy. Table 2.2, therefore, adds to the foregoing figures the roles of the CEO, the top management team, and line managers. Doing so illustrates the organizational complexity that talent management bears.

Table 2.2 illustrates the many actions needed for an organization to implement an effective talent management strategy. Moreover, the table shows how implementation outcome is influenced by the stage of an HR department's evolution. Ideally, the HR area should be leading the implementation process. But this department, as seen in Figures 2.6 and 2.7, can be more operative or more strategic and involved in the business matters according to its development stage. The HR area's degree of development thus directly affects the probability of a successful implementation of a firm's talent management strategy. Finally, Table 2.2 shows the link between the organization's degree of commitment towards the talent management process and the likelihood of successful implementation. It is critical that the talent management process be enhanced to include the involvement of line managers in addition to CEOs and the top management team, as company-wide involvement will increase commitment and facilitate successful implementation. Involvement means, for example, that talent management is on the CEO's agenda, and that he or she and the top management team are participating in the talent reviews and are behind the main strategic decisions and definitions regarding talent within the organization.

The organizational view of talent management is very demanding in that it requires commitment throughout the organization, a well-knit talent management strategy, and a skilled business and talent partner to deploy and implement such a talent management plan.

TABLE 2.2 Where is your organization placed to undertake a talent management strategy?

	No management involvement	Line manager involvement, no CEO and no top management team involvement	Talent management on CEO's agenda	CEO, top management team, and line managers involved
Talent management strategy at organizational level	This scenario is not likely to occur	Without CEO and top management team commitment, the talent management strategy is likely to fail. Human resources is not likely to have the knowledge and savvy to succeed in the implementation	The strategy is likely to need commitment from line managers and the top management team to work	The firm's talent management strategy is likely to be successfully designed and deployed
Talent management strategy focused on an elite group	The talent management strategy is likely to be difficult to implement due to the personnel department not having sufficient skills to undertake the process	Top management team involvement is critical for identifying talent. Human resources is likely to have operational capacity but lacks strategic vision	The strategy is likely to need involvement of managers to ensure effective talent reviews and the identification of talents	An organizational approach to talent management might be required. However, a firm that prefers to focus on an elite group may successfully implement its talent management program

	No management involvement	Line manager involvement, no CEO and no top management team involvement	Talent management on CEO's agenda	CEO, top management team, and line managers involved
Talent management strategy in some areas	The talent management strategy is likely to be difficult to implement due to lack of commitment, organizational interest, and knowledge	Talent management needs to be added to the CEO's agenda, and human resources needs to demonstrate more strategic, forward-looking thinking	The strategy needs to move forward, to include more levels of the organization	While the organization benefits from involvement at various levels, a clear organizational approach is needed
No talent management strategy	Worst-case scenario	A talent management strategy and CEO involvement are required	This scenario is not likely to occur	This scenario is not likely to occur
	Personnel department	**HR department**		**Business and talent partner**

2.2 EFFECTIVE TALENT REVIEWS

Talent reviews are a very important part of the talent management process. A talent review is a process where individuals' role and potential are evaluated in a structured way using various methods. Because an effective talent review includes the top management team, line managers, and HR managers, the review process provides a natural occasion for different organizational layers to become involved in the discussion about the company's talent management aims and processes. Figure 2.9 summarizes the talent review process.

The first step of a talent review is to identify the aims of such a process. Usually, the review process focuses on the objectives set forth when the company designs its talent management program (see chapters 1–2 and section 2.1 to clarify the ways of undertaking this first

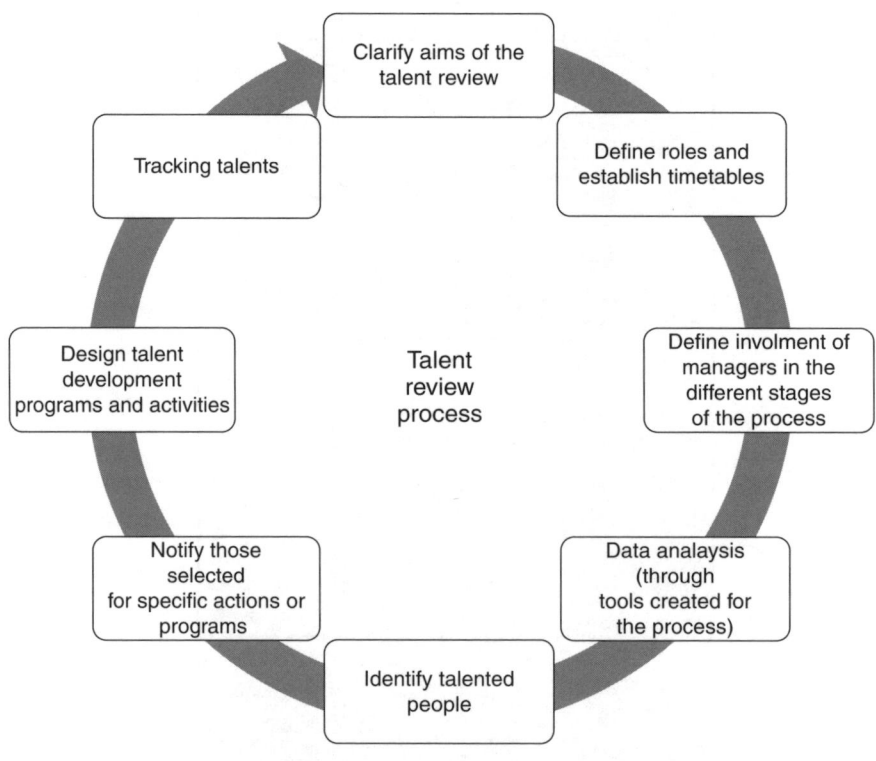

FIGURE 2.9 **The talent review process**

step). By way of example, the goals of a talent review process might include:

- assessing leaders or potential leaders within the company
- defining a succession plan for key leadership positions
- developing talent pools, for example, to create a future leadership pipeline or to meet different business needs
- assessing critical positions to ensure they are filled by high-performance talent
- reviewing talent development plans and vacancy risks.

After identifying the aims of a talent review, a company needs to establish the review's timetable and the roles that different managers will play in the review process. Just as CEO participation, top management team involvement, and line manager accountability are all extremely important to a talent management program's design, they are also important to the talent review process. Varying organizational structures across companies make it hard to specify exactly what role different managers will play in a review. However, generally speaking, the role of different managers will be a function of the leadership level of the position being reviewed. For example, reviews of 'Level 1', 'Level 2', and critical positions within the organization might be overseen by the CEO. The top management team might be involved in a broader scope of reviews, for example, 'Level 1' to 'Level 3' leadership reviews, plus reviews of other critical talents. Line managers may then be responsible for other levels. Figure 2.10 illustrates the managerial involvement in the talent review process. Note that because different managers may be responsible for different or overlapping levels of leadership, it is recommended that those managers involved in the review process meet twice a year for the sake of coherence and consistency (see section 2.1 for more details on roles and responsibilities in the talent management process).

As discussed above, the review process may involve identifying the people who can meet the different needs of the organization, for example, potential successors, emergency replacements, high potentials or critical talent. Inherently, each of these decisions involves identifying the people who can meet these different organizational needs. The organization may decide, however, that some new talent is required and thus, recruitment and selection practices will be of great relevance

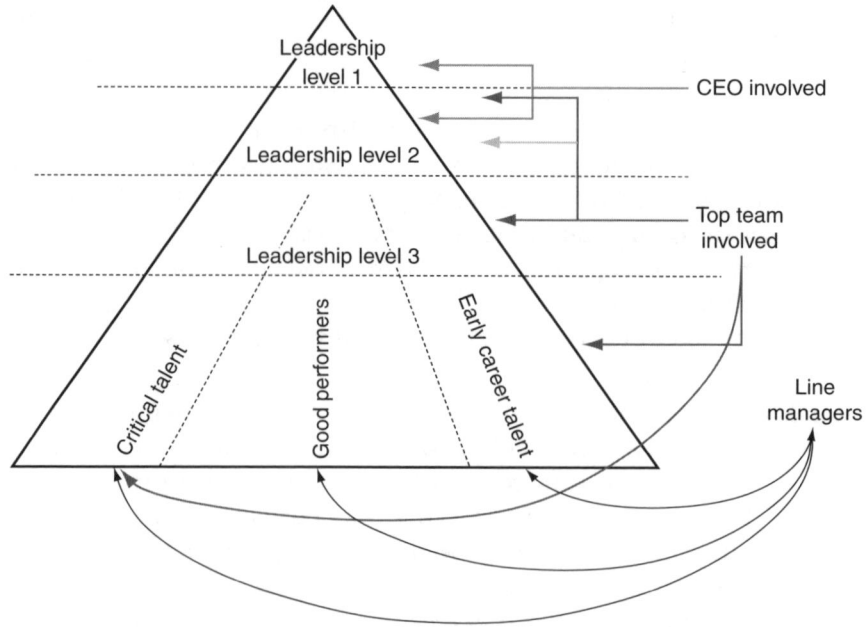

FIGURE 2.10 **Managerial involvement in the talent review process**

(see chapter 3 for a detailed account of recruitment and selection practices).

Thus, the next step in a talent review process is to develop tools that help the firm analyze data and thereby match talent to talent pools or succession plans. The nine-grid box, for example, provides a cross-reference view of current performance versus future potential, and hence helps firms decide who might be a good talent to take into account for a particular pool or program. Figure 2.11 provides a sample nine-grid box; see section 4.1 for a more detailed analysis of this matrix and the identification of talents.

Notifying managers or high potentials who have been selected for specific leadership development activities is the next step in a talent review. As part of this process, the company has to decide when to communicate, and to whom, that a certain person has been chosen to be part of a specific talent pool or a succession plan. On the one hand, notification can increase the retention or commitment of talent pool candidates; on the other hand, however, morale may suffer among non-candidates, leading to problems among employees. As a result, some firms may decide that only high potentials or the managers of

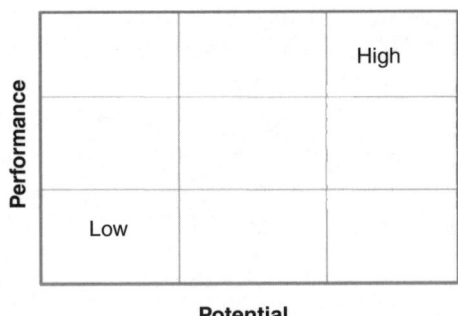

FIGURE 2.11 **Nine-grid box**

high potentials should be notified. Other companies may decide not to release the results of the review at all.

In any case, notifications should be carefully managed, particularly when many people in the company have few leadership development opportunities if they are not in the high potential pool, for example. Put differently, firms should take care to not only identify career paths for high talent individuals, but also for individuals who are not considered for various talent pools. The importance of ensuring that individuals at all levels of the organization have opportunities to take steps forward cannot be overstated. While the possibility of advancement often is a person's driving force in their career, the absence of such possibility can play against motivation and cause the whole process to backfire. Moreover, offering an insufficient range of development programs can produce too wide a separation between those 'who have talent' and those 'who are cast out'. The consequences of such an outcome are obvious: many talented people not being developed, and hence many employees being demotivated and resentful. Notice that advancement opportunities at all levels are tied to the idea that being identified as talented is not something that happens only once for a particular individual, nor is it set in stone. Business needs evolve, as do people's potential and capabilities, as Figure 2.12 illustrates.

Note that an individual's development opportunities are a function of at least three factors:

1) what the employee knows about the company
2) what functions the employee has mastered
3) what the employee's strengths are.

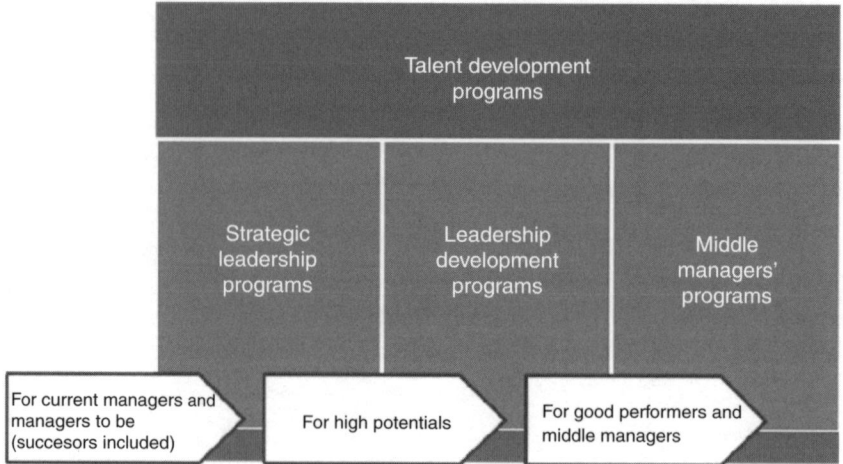

FIGURE 2.12 **Talent development programs**

For an overall development plan to be of much benefit, it has to avoid over-generalizing the programs that it offers; rather, segmentation is needed to take into account differences in employees' career stages and personal needs. For example, two equally talented high potentials with completely different backgrounds and skills will need different development programs to obtain the skills still required to continue moving forward. Therefore, the talent review process has to focus on individuals' real needs in terms of advancement (see section 4.2 for more details on development practices).

During a talent review it is important to assess the retention strategies of the people being reviewed. Understanding individuals' key motivations, identifying projects that present challenges and maintain interest, asking individuals to serve as mentors of other colleagues, and finding other ways for individuals to share their knowledge might help to motivate people. Besides compensation packages, issues related to careers and employability on the one hand and organizational commitment on the other can sometimes be more relevant in the context of today's talent scarcity, rapid organizational change, and macro turbulence. (See chapter 5 for more details on retention strategies.)

Finally, tracking talent is important to be able to record and analyze human capital information such as the movement of employees through the pipeline over time. This requires good-quality human capital metrics to better align talent management techniques and strategies.[3]

To track talented people, it is necessary to match the place in which the person has been located in the potential/performance matrix and the development strategy for each person. People can then be assessed according to different competencies that may indicate the best development plan to follow.

CASE IN POINT: elBulli

elBulli: when talent is ingrained in organizations

What happens when you run an organization in which talent is the basis for success? The case of elBulli, one of the most famous restaurants in the world, illustrates both the importance of individual talent and the relevance of a clear organizational plan regarding talent.

The restaurant, owned and run by Ferran Adrià and Juli Soler since 1990, was first established in 1961 by Hans Schilling and his wife Marketta. Schilling, a homeopathic doctor from Germany, and his wife arrived in Rosas,[4] where they decided to set up the restaurant. Since its inception, the owners have hired talented chefs and staff to make sure that the gastronomy of the restaurant continues to move forward. Jean-Louis Neichel, Jean-Paul Vinay, and Christian Lutaud were among the chefs under the founders' ownership. The founders' ambition, plus that of the current owners, has led the restaurant to be voted 'Best restaurant in the world' four times by an international panel of chefs and food critics for *Restaurant Magazine*, one of the most sought-after accolades in the restaurant industry.[5] In addition, the restaurant was awarded its first Michelin star in 1976, its second in 1990, and its third in 1997.[6]

Every year, elBulli receives approximately 2 million reservation requests but only 8000 can be satisfied. That translates into roughly 50 people a day, over some 160 days a year. And the rest of the year?

'The restaurant,' states Ferran Adrià, 'opens six months a year, this is because you need more time to create'.[7] Adrià and his creative team work six months in a Barcelona workshop in which they continuously develop new cooking techniques and concepts. This search is, for Adrià, the highest level of creativity. Developing techniques is the focus of the winter creative sessions at the elBulli workshop.

This search for new techniques and concepts at elBulli has resulted in major discoveries and minor developments alike. Examples include the frozen savory world, non-pasta ravioli, sperification (tiny flavored spheres of vegetables or fruits), caramelization, foams, hot jellies, and many more gastronomic inventions that have created a *new nouvelle cuisine*):

Left: Spherical ravioli of peas and minty pea salad.
Center: Frozen Parmesan air with muesli.
Right: Hibiscus paper with blackcurrant and eucalyptus.
Courtesy: elBulli. Photos Francesc Guillamet

'Cooking is not difficult. Creating, however, is another thing altogether', notes Adrià. 'While you create you need to get out of the routine and be aware of creative rhythm. This creative rhythm tells you when you have to change, explore or exploit things.'[8] 'Creativity means not copying': this definition of creativity, given by the chef Jacques Maximin, inspired Ferran Adrià to take a new radical approach. 'This idea [Maxim's phrase] was the spark that started the creative fire of Adrià and he started to forge his own creative direction.'[9]

Of course, while a focus on individual talent has been critical to elBulli's success in procuring the creativity needed, an organizational point of view has also been important to align the values of the organization and the talent required. At the restaurant there are 30 to 40 chefs, depending on the season. Of these, 13 are full time and the rest are 'stagers'. The stagers are chosen from among those applicants that have contacted the restaurant. Says Marc Cuspinera, Personnel Manager and Consulting Business Manager: 'We are lucky to have more than 5000 requests per year for fewer than 35 places to work here. At the same time this is a tough job and a responsibility as well. You need to decide the correct profile and select those who would like to work here and who will fit our organizational culture.'

Left: afternoon meeting or *mise en scène*. The creative team introduces the new dishes and discusses any improvements to be made.
Right: chefs and stagers prepare the 1,500 cocktails, snacks, tapas dishes, avant desserts, desserts, and morphings served each day.

Selection criteria are all-important. Stagers are selected from many countries so that the kitchen can benefit from the knowledge and experience of their native countries.[10] But there are other criteria as well, as some members of the elBulli team highlighted: experience, teamwork, and engagement. Regarding the experience needed, Marc Cuspinera, asserted: 'We need to level up the members of the team so that experience is balanced out. That is why we prefer people with a certain experience.'

Teamwork and engagement are also critical aspects for being part of such a select team, as Mateu Casañas, Head Chef, explains. 'Creativity here never stops, one idea develops and we move forward. In this context you will not say "this is mine", we expect people to work for the same objective. Generosity is critical to be part of this team.' Indeed, generosity and openness are important parts of the creative method at elBulli. Each new technique at elBulli is documented and published. The idea behind this is that the discoveries made at elBulli can help worldwide cuisine evolve and develop. 'My secret is not to have secrets,' comments Adrià in the book *elBulli Desde Dentro*. 'At elBulli we are moved by creativity and our wish to innovate' (Moret, 2007). As such, academics such as Sandulli & Chesbrough (2009) consider elBulli to be part of a group of companies with an open system model. One of the main features of firms with such a model of doing business is to generate knowledge and share it.[11]

Left: Ferrán Adrià (left) and chef Oriol Castro (center) in the process of innovation.
Right: waiters are gathered before the meeting. In this meeting, waiters learn who will be dining at the restaurant, new dishes or changes, and the way a dish has to be served. Feedback on new dishes is also discussed. (Marc Cuspinera – with white apron – sits in the middle.)

At the end of the stagers' time with elBulli, they have gained more than gastronomic knowledge: 'People here learn not only recipes, but also a new way of working. Here we have many different things you can learn, such as the way we run an organization,' says Marc Cuspinera.

Alejandro Digilio, an ex-stager, commented on his own experience at elBulli: 'The experience of working at elBulli was a turning point in my professional career. Once you arrive you are in shock because of the perfectionism, precision, and thoroughness required to have the job done. But you learn, not only about "cuisine" but you also learn to be rigorous, serious, and demanding; to be able to be the best in your field. The experience to be one of them for a while, you cannot learn it in books. It is a thrilling time.'[12]

In summary, at elBulli individual talent should be matched with a strong creative team to enhance the possibilities for learning at both the individual and the organizational level. Cuspinera further underscores the importance of having the right talent: 'It would be a mistake for someone to come here if he or she believes that the first day they will learn and take just recipes. That person did not understand that this is an organization in which we share time, generosity, and knowledge. And it would have been our mistake to have hired such a talent because that individual talent is not leveraging the organizational talent we need to develop.'

CHAPTER HIGHLIGHTS

❖ Talent refers to the skills or capabilities people have that enable them to perform a certain task. Talent can be found at each level of the organization.

❖ Talent management is a strategic activity that is aligned with the firm's business strategy and aims at attracting, developing, and retaining people at each level of the organization.

❖ Talent management emphasizes the importance of talent as an organizational capability.

❖ A talent mindset requires the engagement of the entire organization, not just the HR department. The CEO, top management team, and line managers should be responsible and accountable for the design and implementation of a company's talent management program.

❖ Human resources facilitates the talent management process and is involved in strategic talent decisions. Human resources should strive to become a talent and business partner.

VERY IMPORTANT QUESTIONS

☉ Is there a common understanding in your organization of what talent is?

☉ Does your organization require an individual or an organizational approach towards talent?

- Should talent management focus on an elite group or should it be an inclusive concept?
- Is talent management a strategic priority for the CEO and top management team?
- Do the CEO and top management team have a talent agenda?
- Are line managers committed to the talent management process?

  - Are they enablers of, or barriers to, talent development?

- Is talent management the strategic driving force behind the HR department?

  - Is the HR department facilitating this process?

3

TALENT MANAGEMENT STEP 1: ATTRACTING THE RIGHT TALENT

In searching for talent, identifying a skilled candidate is not enough. Rather, the company also has to consider factors such as what type of talent is needed for a position or which organizational capabilities it would like the position to enhance.

Understanding which organizational capabilities the firm needs to develop for future sustainability and success will certainly influence the match between a position and employees' or candidates' skills. For example, companies that seek to enhance their organizational flexibility in order to better compete in a hypercompetitive environment (D'Aveni, 1994; Volberda, 1999; Hatum, 2007) may try to build organizations comprised of people with diverse backgrounds, so that fresh ideas can flow into the firm and new strategic initiatives can emerge that help the company anticipate competitors' moves (Hatum & Pettigrew, 2006).

However, to attract the best people for the company, a firm should do more than simply analyze its organizational competencies and determine what types of talent are required. First, it is important that the company has an employee value proposition (EVP). An EVP summarizes what employees can expect to receive from the company in exchange for the work they perform. As such, an EVP is the set of benefits that characterize an employer. A good EVP enhances the company's reputation as a good place to work, and thus drives talent attraction and retention. Second, an organization needs to identify which recruitment channels are most appropriate to attract the desired talent according to its cultural and organizational characteristics, and which selection practices are most likely to help the firm identify a good candidate for a given position. That is, the organization needs to identify the staffing processes that will help it achieve its talent goals.

This chapter explores these and related issues that are fundamental to attracting the right talent.

3.1 THE EMPLOYEE VALUE PROPOSITION (EVP): DREAMS COME TRUE

Michaels et al. (2001, p. 43) define an EVP as the 'holistic sum of everything people experience and receive while they are part of a company – everything from the intrinsic satisfaction of the work to the environment, leadership, colleagues, compensation, and more. It's about how well the company fulfils people's needs, their expectations, and even their dreams.' Continuing, the authors observe that 'a strong EVP attracts great people like flowers attract bees'.

For the purpose of this book an EVP comprises the firm's organizational features that allow it to promote itself outwardly and generate loyalty internally. *Organizational features* refer to the following four sets of characteristics:

1) the firm's *organizational culture* (e.g., entrepreneurial spirit, risk-taking attitude, corporate social responsibility policy)
2) the firm's *people* (e.g., degree of teamwork, leadership style)
3) the firm's *work* characteristics (e.g., the extent of innovation, the degree of work–life balance)
4) the *rewards* the firm offers (e.g., compensation, perks, long-term incentives).

Figure 3.1 shows the four dimensions or characteristics of the EVP as explained above.

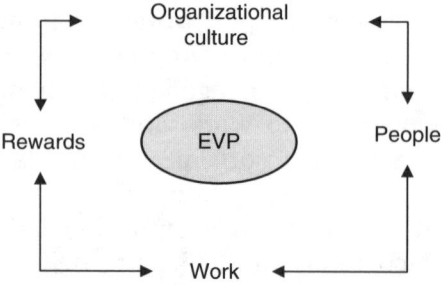

FIGURE 3.1 **The dimensions of an EVP**

Note that an EVP is related to employer branding (Lawler III, 2008; Thorne & Pellant, 2007; Davis et al., 2007; Hieronimus, et al., 2005). An employer brand describes the uniqueness of the organization, or the organization's 'cultural personality' (Cheese et al., 2008, p. 100). However, an EVP is more comprehensive than an employer brand in that the EVP reflects an experience or a way of life.

The EVP is a means of conveying individuals' feelings and experiences at their workplace. The EVP competes in the market with other EVPs or brands to attract the best talent. As Davis et al. (2007) argue, organizations should have a brand soul that conveys three messages about the company: the company is a good company to work for, a company to stay with, and a company building for the future. Such a brand creates 'an emotional bond' (Rueff & Stringer, 2006, p. 63). It is this emotional bond that helps the company compete against other companies to attract top talent. Moreover, unlike an employer brand, the emotional bond of an EVP can help the company retain talented recruits once they are on board. Thus, effective EVPs not only deliver a message that helps attract prospective employees, but also actions and behaviors that are attractive to those already working within the organization.

To see how a company's EVP can work to create an emotional bond with potential or current employees, consider the well-designed EVP of Johnson & Johnson (J&J), a company with more than 120,000 employees and 250 companies worldwide that operates in three business segments (consumer products, medical devices and diagnostics, and pharmaceuticals). On its webpage, the bottom-line message conveyed to prospective employees is clear: 'small-company environment, big-company impact'. Using the framework of the four organizational features listed above, further analysis of J&J's website reveals how the company seeks to clearly deliver on this value proposition to talent that is already on board.[1] Looking at the firm's *organizational culture*, it is possible to see that J&J emphasizes a decentralized corporate structure, offering a small company environment but with the potential for huge impact, and a value-based culture. The *people* dimension emphasizes a collaborative and team-based work environment; honesty, integrity, and passion are also highlighted. The *work* dimension highlights opportunities for employees to develop career paths across companies, functions, and positions. Finally, the *rewards* dimension highlights the flexible choices that support employees' short-term and long-term financial goals, and various work-, family- and personal-life programs that are an outcome of the business culture.

It cannot be overstated how important a powerful EVP can be for attracting talent. Just ask any university graduate or MBA student which consultancy firm they would most like to work for, and McKinsey or BCG (Boston Consulting Group) would be at the top of the list. Graduate students see these firms as being very selective in terms of who they hire and in terms of which projects they choose to undertake – as exclusive clubs whose members are those privileged to be invited by the firms. Once you are on board, you get the opportunity for 'exceptional professional and personal growth'.[2]

So how can a company strengthen its EVP so that it can compete more effectively against others in the market? The Royal Mail Group,[3] the largest employer in the UK, provides an example. Royal Mail's goal was to make sure that divergent thinking took place throughout the organization. The firm believed that differences in thinking would generate better performance than in a context where everyone shared similar thinking. Toward this end, the firm conducted a diversity review, which led the company to understand how it was positioned in the market and how to attract people that might be a good fit, as related to its diversity goal. In the case of the graduate program, which Royal Mail uses to identify more than 100 new recruits every year, the company determined which aspects of the Royal Mail brand to emphasize in order to attract a diverse set of graduates. Those aspects identified included: corporate social responsibility activities (e.g., the company's energy reduction programs, well-being initiatives, and charity events); the challenging opportunities one may be able to work on at the company; and the history of Royal Mail, a firm that has been around since Henry VIII created the 'Master of Posts'.[4] This analysis made it possible for Royal Mail to offer to the prospective young candidates 'opportunity, variety, location and flexibility'.[5]

More generally, several questions need to be addressed in order to build a stronger EVP:

- Which elements of your company's organizational culture, work characteristics, people, and rewards are seen by prospective or current employees as a positive aspect of working for the company?
- Which of these elements does your company offer more reliably than other firms, that is, which of these elements are competitive strengths?

- What is the compelling story that can be communicated to people about working in your organization?
- Which elements are unattractive and need to be changed or replaced? Do any elements of your company's current EVP undermine attraction or retention?
- Does your company incorporate any of the firm's organizational values in the EVP?
- Is your company's EVP aligned with the firm's business strategy?
- What about the competition? How does your company's EVP compare with others in the industry?

The resulting EVP needs to be concrete and convincing: in addition to understanding what the company does, people need to understand what it is like to work for the company. Furthermore, the EVP needs to be realistic and consistent so that the company does not have to amend its position, for doing so could damage the firm's reputation, particularly since employees and ex-employees have ample opportunity to comment on the Web about the company's management. Consider, for example, reading a comment such as: 'Badly disorganized with no leadership from management or above...'[6] Such a remark would be difficult to swallow. Therefore, the following question posed by Martin et al. (2005, p. 79) regarding employer branding is important to take into consideration: 'How do we tell the story to potential and existing employees in a way that convinces them of the reality of what we have to offer?'

Best practices at a glance

Southwest Airlines: LUV'ing it

Southwest Airlines is the world's most successful low-fare, point-to-point, high-frequency carrier. The company operates approximately 3400 flights a day between 64 cities, using more than 540 Boeing 737 aircraft. Year-end results for 2008 marked Southwest's 36th consecutive year of profitability, a rarity in an industry generally characterized by severe financial crisis. These profits were based on operating revenues of US$11 bn and a net income of US$294 m, with a total of 101.9 million passengers carried.[7] As a result of its high-quality service and persistent performance, the company has received numerous awards, including friendliest airline (Time.com survey), a top shareholder-friendly company (*Institutional Investor* magazine), and a

---

(Continued)

most admired airline (Fortune). What is it about Southwest that sets it apart from its peers?

Founded by Herb Kelleher in 1971, the 'LUV' (or love) airline is well known for its friendly and caring atmosphere, and for a high level of employee commitment, customer satisfaction, and productivity. The company is further known for its creative marketing campaigns that reinforce the firm's 'nutty' brand image (Freiberg & Freiberg, 1998). However, the company advertisements and website also present a coherent EVP.

In particular, Southwest's 'Symbol of Freedom' campaign communicates the company's commitment to customers' freedom to fly, by offering low-cost fares and ensuring a freedom from fees.[8] Importantly, however, the same freedom from hassle offered to customers is also offered to employees in the performance of their jobs. For instance, Southwest's EVP includes a commitment to employees' freedom to work hard and have fun, to create and innovate, to pursue good health, and to create financial security: 'We have a legendary past, a bright future, and a simple mission to give America the freedom to fly.'[9]

In a 2008 interview Libby Sartain, a former HR manager at Southwest, noted that for Southwest to deliver quality service to customers, it was important for employees to believe in the idea of the 'Symbol of Freedom', and that one's experience working at Southwest was the corner-stone for developing such a connection: '[As employees,] we had the freedom to learn and grow, the freedom to create financial security, the freedom to work hard and have fun...' Then, through the overall employee brand, 'At Southwest, freedom begins with me,' 'we made that connection that you're delivering the freedom that Southwest delivers you, the employee, and in turn you get these freedoms from working here.'[10]

The company's communications express the central role of employees: 'Our people are our single greatest strength and our most enduring longterm competitive advantage.'[11] By communicating to its internal customers and prospective employees the values of freedom, along with customer service, the company ensures that people who share those values and are likely to succeed at Southwest find the right place to work at the company.

After designing a strong EVP, the company is ready to turn its attention to the next critical step in the talent search process: the staffing process.

3.2 STAFFING: THE RECRUITING AND SELECTION PROCESSES

The extent to which the company's EVP acts as a filter in attracting those candidates that are likely to be a good fit for the firm demonstrates how effective the EVP truly is. However, an effective EVP alone cannot ensure that the company will ultimately hire the best talent. Rather, the company's staffing processes, that is, its recruitment and selection processes, are critical to ultimately hiring the right personnel. Thus, while well-organized staffing processes can make the investment that goes into crafting the EVP worth its weight in gold, poorly organized staffing processes will leave the company back at square one, causing the organization to lose both time and money.

In developing their staffing processes, companies should consider which industries they are in and what processes their competitors are using. Moreover, companies should seek not only to fill current vacancies within their organizations, but also broaden their scope by searching for additional talent so as to be able to pump real talent at all levels of the organization (Michaels et al., 2001). This is essential at senior and middle-management levels of the organization. It is also important to identify high potentials.

The focus on searching broadly for talent entails setting aside the dichotomy of promoting from within versus promoting from outside – the organization needs to do both. While incumbents offer experience and stability in terms of corporate views and processes, new people often have different ideas, values, and ways of thinking, and in turn bring about more discussion, opposite perspectives and change. While the factors associated with new recruits may lead to some conflict, a firm that overcomes this process will be able to attract the truly talented and, hence, will be better equipped to overtake its competitors.

The literature on top management teams and cognitive processes suggests the importance of the cognitive diversity of the top management team (Wiersema & Bantel, 1992). For instance, according to Hambrick & Mason's (1984) seminal paper on the role and influence of the top management team in organizations, heterogeneous managers interpret reality from a different cognitive base, with different visions and managerial perceptions. As a result, the decision-making process of a team comprised of heterogeneous managers is more likely to contain a greater number of innovative alternatives than a team of more homogeneous managers. This argument finds support in various theories that suggest that the existence of different mental models in an organization might enhance the organization's ability to adapt to change, enhancing the capacity for action (Greenwood & Hinnings, 1996) or action orientation in an organization (Grinyer et al., 1988). Over time this capacity for action will boost the firm's risk-taking behavior. The capacity for action can be seen in those firms and managers willing to explore new strategic alternatives, the eagerness of firms to take risks, and the enthusiasm with which the top management team confronts difficult issues (Hatum, 2007; Webb & Pettigrew, 1999; Greenwood & Hinnings, 1996).

Notice that another implication of searching broadly for talent, rather than searching to fill vacant positions, is that companies will find desirable talent for which there may not be an immediate position. Indeed, by creating talent pools in this way, organizations will be able to put people into positions in which they can develop, in preparation to take over more important positions as these become vacant. This idea of managing the scarce resource that is talent by means of talent pools will be explained later in the book.

Figure 3.2 depicts the differences between a 'hiring to fill vacant positions' view of staffing and a view based on hiring when talent is identified and then finding the ideal position for the individual ('hire first, find the position second').

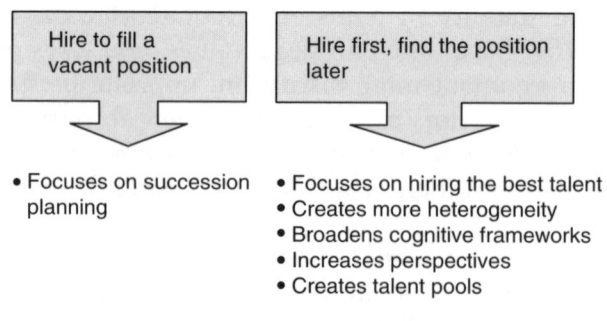

FIGURE 3.2 **Why hire?**

So, what are the best recruitment processes to use to attract the best talent for your organization?

3.2.1 Recruiting: thinking broadly and segmenting

Many years ago, recruiting wasn't terribly complex. Michaels et al. (2001) and Sears (2003) describe a historical business situation that sheds light on the early scale and scope of a personnel department. When, in 1914, Henry Ford decided to double salaries at his plant in Michigan (from US$2.50 to US$5), people began to queue overnight. In response, the personnel department had the candidates fill out forms and then it interviewed the candidates. HR's role thus amounted to making job descriptions and designing processes and procedures to best capture the strengths of prospective employees (Sears, 2003). Meanwhile, all interested candidates were considered.

If you think that recruiting continues to be this easy, think again. Scarcity in different sectors has made this process more complicated. Employees have become selective and demanding. And technology, while automating some processes, has further worked to increase the complexity of the processes themselves. Thus, at some point, recruitment began to be a critical process in staffing the organization. In contrast to Ford in 1914, the aim today is not to attract all possible candidates, but rather to attract the talent that the organization needs. This is done in part by means of the company's EVP. Of course, the company will need to adapt the message of the EVP to the different pools of employees sought. Thus, seeking good talent requires segmenting the market by the message the company conveys through its EVP.

Why is customizing the EVP to target different segments so important? In short, segmenting is important because of the demographic changes discussed at the beginning of this book that have affected the labor market. The three generations presently co-existing in the labor market (Baby Boomers, Gen X, and Gen Y) have different aspirations and values. Thus, when approaching the market to recruit, organizations should take this demographic diversity into account by segmenting accordingly. For example, Tesco, a large supermarket chain in the UK with operations worldwide, divides its recruitment into two groups – one for graduates and the other for students – tailoring its messages according to the needs of each group (Guthridge et al., 2008; see http://www.tesco-careers.com). The idea is that by segmenting the company's needs, members of each segment can find their own place within the firm.

As the next section of this book will demonstrate, the use of segmenting to take different needs into account can also help companies decide which recruiting channel is best able to attract the most qualified people for the organization's needs.

Off the record

Chasing Gen Y: attracting it might be more difficult than expected (even during a crisis)

'I don't want to work 40 hours a week' or 'I want to wear informal clothing and work in a relaxed and informal atmosphere' are now common for managers to hear from the Millennial Generation, also known as Gen Y. In many cases, managers were outraged when they first encountered the attitude and apparent arrogance of Gen Y. However, such views have been revealed to be common among the new generation. Gen Y has great expectations regarding work issues, such as higher pay, flexible work schedules, rapid promotion, and more personal time. Gen Y judges that it can afford to be selective. Why? The answer is twofold.

First, Gen Y is aware that the Baby Boomers are close to retirement and as Berke et al. (2008, p. 1) note, 'when the older workers leave, there simply will not be enough trained managers and executives for some time'. Second, Millennials are primarily Baby Boomers' children that have seen their parents give away their time, and life, to organizations that later 'betrayed' them by firing them.

These 'Trophy Kids', as lately defined by Alsop (2008), are the pride and joy of their parents who praised them lavishly when they excelled. As a result, Gen Y'ers place a high premium on success and achievement. These 'Kids', however, may bring to an organization a whole new set of capabilities that can be important when competition intensifies and the marketplace is in turmoil: they can be hard workers if they are engaged by the project, they are good at juggling many tasks at once, and they are savvy regarding internet technology.

A recent article[12] on Gen Y and the economic downturn highlights the importance of this generation to tackling the recession. The article cites how Best Buy, a big American consumer-electronics retailer, was able to save money and boost sales using the help of a small group of Gen Y'ers eager to innovate and be creative. In the midst of a deep economic downturn, one might expect Millennials to be more inclined to comprise with respect to their usual demands. But to the extent this may be the case, it is just as likely that once the market bounces back the ingrained trait this generation brings with it will surface swiftly.

Certainly, these knowledge worker talents, as Terjesen & Viola Frei (2008) call Gen Y, are not easy to convince but they might be worth trying.

Best practices at a glance

Cirque du Soleil: treasure hunting and creative transformation[13]

CIRQUE DU SOLEIL.

With 19 shows performing around the world and plans to expand to 22 shows worldwide by the end of 2010, searching for talent is not only important, but critical for *Cirque du Soleil*:[14]

The Canadian firm has around 4000 employees from 40 nations that together speak 25 languages.[15] *Cirque du Soleil* has brought wonder and delight to almost 90 million spectators in over 200 cities on 5 continents.[16] *Cirque du Soleil* is famous for reinventing the traditional circus – it is a circus without animals. The firm's performance and flair can only be compared to Broadway musicals. This creation was considered by Kim & Mauborgne (2005) a blue ocean strategy, because *Cirque du Soleil* created a whole new circus experience and a market that did not exist at that moment. By creating a new market in a space that previously did not exist, *Cirque du Soleil* effectively made competition irrelevant.

Yet the need to engage in recruiting is far from trivial. Thinking broadly is a good way to characterize the recruiting activities at *Cirque du Soleil*. Recruiters at the organization scout the world for talent. Recruiting is a twofold activity: recruiters look for both talented people and people who bring new ideas and inspiration. While seeking ideas and seeking talent might be a good combination for a highly creative company, together these goals make the search process more complicated. The 15 professional recruiters of the company's casting department scout the world for talent. This search process entails looking everywhere from circus festivals to dance festivals, music festivals, swimming championships, world diving championships, and the Olympic Games.[17] It is, therefore, rather extensive and time-consuming. However, by broadening the scope of the recruiting process, and going where no other competitors go (or to more places than potential competitors can go) to search for talent, *Cirque du Soleil* has the advantage of a diverse workforce of artistes that add originality and creativity to its shows.

3.2.1.1 Recruitment channels

The recruitment channels that an organization will use to contact potential candidates will depend on the organization's target employees. However, it is important that the various channels used send a consistent message that is in line with the realities that employees face at the company, as otherwise new recruits will eventually leave the company, resulting in increased turnover and, in turn, a loss on the investment in recruiting.

Here follows an analysis of various recruitment channels available to firms as they seek to identify those candidates that are likely to be a good match for the firm.

Employee referrals

In referral programs, employees submit the names of candidates for various positions. Such programs can be open (i.e., the company receives CVs that feed into a database; if a referred candidate is chosen, the referring employee is awarded money or some other recognition), or specific (i.e., the firm receives referrals for positions that have been posted).

Google (the internet content provider) is one company in which its best employees have been hired through referrals. On its web page, the company states that if a referral accepts an offer and stays at the company for at least 60 days, the referring employee will receive a bonus.[18] According to the New York Job Source,[19] this can be as high as US$2000. Such a value highlights the importance Google gives to this type of employee sourcing.

Company website

A company's website can be an excellent tool for sourcing candidates; however, it is not always used in an efficient way. Many companies have a 'career section' on their website but its sole purpose is to receive stacks of CVs. Ideally, a firm's website should be used to attract people who are interested in the company's career opportunities and development possibilities.

An example of a company that makes good use of its career website is Procter & Gamble (P&G; http://www.pg.com). While P&G's career web page allows people to send in their CVs, it tests them at the same time.

In particular, P&G's sophisticated online application process includes an assessment of applicants' capabilities through specific questions that will enable the candidate to pass through certain steps of the hiring process. This process is known in the company as the 'steps to succeed: the hiring process'.[20] Moreover, P&G makes intensive use of its career web page by centralizing recruitment globally, helping candidates find a job that suits them no matter where they are located.

Universities/business schools

Recruiters wanting younger talent must turn to universities and business schools. However, this form of scouting has changed greatly over the past ten years. Previously, multinationals visited the top ten business schools, for example, making a presentation and interviewing those individuals that they thought were the best candidates for the firm. Today a different approach is followed. Students are being more selective and demanding, making the recruitment process more difficult for companies. In response, some firms have started to segment the universities, broadening the scope of the search by considering specializations or locations. This seems to be an intelligent idea, although it can be very tiresome for the recruiter. A report published by the Boston Consultancy Group[21] finds that the best graduates from less well-known schools are frequently more motivated and loyal than those from the elite schools. Consistent with this idea, the same report notes that Tata Consultancy Services in India has developed strong ties with less-renowned schools in order to access the best students, even offering extra training to students and faculty alike.

Another factor to consider in relation to this recruitment channel is which region the company is trying to recruit from. In the US, many universities offer MBA programs, and recruiting at the MBA level has a long tradition. In other parts of the world, for example, Latin America, this is not the case. The Executive MBA is a highly valued form of postgraduate training for those with a few years' work experience who want to climb the corporate ladder.

e-recruiting

This recruitment channel is widely used by both firms and candidates. The most important 'job boards' are Monster (http://www.monster.com), Career Builder (http://www.careerbuilder.com) and Yahoo! HotJobs (http://hotjobs.yahoo.com). Although these are among the most important resources to use when pursuing an e-recruiting strategy, they are often insufficient to satisfy an organization's recruiting needs. In markets such as the oil industry, where talent is particularly scarce, niche boards such as http://www.rigzone.com or http://www.oilcareers.com better serve those niches or industries where there is a dearth of specialists.

In addition, companies can profit from turning to social networks as part of their e-recruiting efforts. Sites such as LinkedIn (http://www.linkedin.com) and Jobster (http://www.jobster.com) lead these networks for finding professionals. On the other hand, Facebook (http://www.facebook.com) and Hi5 (http://www.hi5.com) can be used to target younger people and students.

Online simulations

In recent years, some companies have started using simulation tests that aim to assess individuals' real capabilities. Such tests also allow firms to attract a particular segment of people, namely, undergraduates and MBAs. For example, P&G has a simulation called Just in Case (http://www.pgjustincase.com) that works as a virtual case study. The simulation tests an individual's ability to develop a product or a project in one hour. Candidates compete between themselves online. L'Oréal has also been a frontrunner in the use of business simulations as part of its online recruiting. Indeed, L'Oréal's e-Strat challenge (http://www.e-strat.loreal.com) is one of the most important of its kind. Launched in 2000 during the internet boom, e-Strat aims to attract profiles of potential candidates (both undergraduates and MBAs) from around the world. The candidate's objective is to manage an international portfolio of products for a two-month period. Since the simulation started, 221,000 students from 2200 business schools and universities from 128 countries have participated in the competition.[22]

Other business simulations in the market used for testing and recruiting include Danone's Trust, IBM's UBC Challenge, and McKinsey's Euroacademy. In addition, some business games are multi-sponsored, such as Euromanager (sponsored by PriceWaterhouseCoopers, Microsoft, and HSBC, among others), Global Business Challenge (sponsored by HP, Starbucks, Ford Motors, and Boeing), and SIFE World Cup (sponsored by Walmart, Coca-Cola, Nestlé, and Unilever, among others). In the future these online simulations are likely to become standard practice and a key tool for recruiting.

Advertisement of L'Oréal e.strat, the business simulation used by the company
Picture: Courtesy L'Oréal Company

Video résumé and other online channels

This new era of talent in which people choose which jobs or companies they would like to work with has paved the way for the video résumé to appear in the market. Through the use of sites such as YouTube (http://www.youtube.com), prospective employees are now able to introduce and sell themselves online, and many young professionals (or not so young) can communicate not only their experience but also their wishes in very creative ways.

Two other possible vehicles for e-recruiting include Second Life (http://www.secondlife.com), a virtual world for socializing and reinventing yourself,[23] and blogs. Of the two, blogs are more frequently used for recruitment purposes. For example, Globant, an offshore IT outsourcing firm with offices in Latin America, the UK, and the US, uses blogs to do what it calls 'fly-fishing'. The recruitment team leaves technical questions that are difficult to answer in blogs that they know their targets visit. Those individuals who answer the questions correctly are then invited to participate in the selection process.

Advertisement used by Globat using the method of fly-fishing
Picture: Courtesy Globant

Best practices at a glance

Recruitment by direct sourcing: Red 5 Studios[24]

A June 2007 *Wall Street Journal* article illustrates the power of direct recruiting:

Four months ago, a FedEx box landed on the desk of Scott Youngblood, a videogame designer working in Bend, Ore. Inside, he found a glossy box nestled in thick foam. Inside that box was another and, within that one, another.

Eventually, Mr Youngblood opened five boxes, nested Russian-doll style, and discovered an iPod shuffle music player engraved with his name. He pressed play and heard the voice of Mark Kern, president and chief executive of online videogame maker Red 5 Studios Inc., talking about Mr Youngblood's past work on games and inviting him to a web site to learn more about Red 5. 'I was blown away,' says Mr Youngblood. Within two weeks, he interviewed at Red 5. And a little over a month later, he started a new job there – leaving his position at Sony Corp's Sony Computer Entertainment America and moving more than 800 miles away.

Mr Youngblood's package was one of 100 that Red 5 sent to its 'dream hires', identified through a concerted recruiting campaign. Four months after the recruiting effort launched, three of the candidates have joined the Aliso Viejo, Calif., upstart while one is currently interviewing. An industry buzz about the campaign has helped to raise the company's profile.

One might notice that the recruitment channels discussed above do not comprise an exhaustive list. For the sake of brevity, this book has left aside more traditional channels such as headhunting, which are also important to a company's overall recruitment strategy, focusing instead on more innovative trends in the recruitment field. The 'newness' of some of these methods should not lure the HR professional or recruiter away from traditional recruitment channels, however. Rather, each company should explore whether some of the new channels may help improve the recruitment of some target segment or another. For instance, when revising the portfolio of channels used, companies should take into account the company's culture, the company's EVP, and how the EVP's message will be communicated. Companies with a more traditional culture may focus more on direct referrals to make sure new recruits are right for the firm's culture. More innovative firms that compete in hypercompetitive markets may need to incorporate e-recruitment or simulations into their recruitment processes. And when talent is scarce, companies may be required to pursue numerous strategies, using headhunting, industry job boards, and even professional associations, to ensure they have scouted the market far and wide.

Once an organization's recruiting process has been decided, the next step is to determine which selection methods to use. Several questions are relevant to this process. For instance: Which methods are best for selecting talent under the strain of talent scarcity? Do we have to interview? What sort of interview is required or recommended? The next section discusses some of ideas and methods that are relevant to successfully selecting talent.

3.2.2 Selecting the best: tricks and traps

When looking for talent, organizations tend to focus their attention on sourcing, that is, on how to identify candidates. However, after candidates have been identified, the selection process starts. It is at this juncture that problems often arise, mainly because companies fail to align their selection process with specific organizational needs. In particular, notwithstanding how sophisticated the selection process may be, this process often fails to match candidates' suitability for the position or the organization's culture.

Snow & Snell (1993) underscore the strategic importance of the staffing model that is employed to select talent. Baron et al. (1996) further emphasize the critical role of the selection process. Indeed, in their analysis of start-ups, Baron and his associates establish that the blueprint of an emergent organization is influenced by three dimensions: the basis of attachment, the means of control, and the criteria of selection. Baron et al. (1996) show that the impact of selection is so great that it can change the characteristics of the firm. Baron et al. argue that organizations should therefore select people taking into consideration three different criteria: skills, potential, and the extent to which the candidate fits with the organization.

Among other factors, network and group dynamics should be considered when hiring. Groysberg et al. (2004, 2006) find that when a company hires a star, the star's performance plunges and the group's dynamics decline. This suggests that companies may not find it desirable to always hire stars. In a large longitudinal study of semiconductor firms operating in high-velocity environments, Eisenhardt & Schoonhoven (1990) further highlight the importance of the top team having worked together before. Those teams with a shared history were more able to survive turmoil. Thus, if a firm is hiring a star, the firm should also focus on hiring members of his team or network so that the person will perform better and be able to make decisions quickly and effectively, avoiding frictions due to inertia among the firm's current employees.

The selection process is important. However, before initiating the hiring process, a company should determine why the organization is hiring in the first place as the firm's hiring goals may suggest which selection methods to use. For example, if the company is looking for an experienced manager it may employ one selection method, but if it is looking to hire younger talent it may employ a different method. Alternatively, a firm that seeks to identify people who will be a good fit with its culture might choose yet another selection method. Thus, determining the reason for a talent search is an important first step to

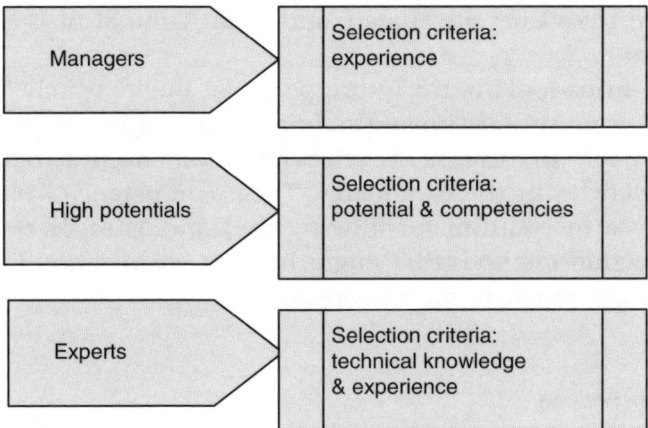

FIGURE 3.3 **Example of selection criteria by pools of talent**

choosing the right selection methods, something that is particularly important in this era in which staffing is expensive and recruiting and hiring take longer. Moreover, in today's market, organizations need to customize their selection criteria. Before, when talent management was not a big concern, firms could afford to have only one criterion that they modified slightly depending on the status or role of the person being selected. In the current environment, in contrast, firms need to identify those practices and methods that ensure they are hiring the right talent. Figure 3.3 shows how a company's selection criteria may vary across different groups, or pools, of talent.

For example, if the selection criterion is experience, the organization may require the candidate to bring certain aptitudes, technical expertise, and/or skills to the organization. In this case the organization needs to inquire about the candidate's past performance to make sure that the person has the right mix of experience to meet the company's needs.

Another possible selection criterion might focus on the candidate's organizational fit in terms of his or her attitude. This would be appropriate when the values and culture of the organization are so strong that the candidate will need to not only perform well but also adapt to the work environment to be successful in his or her position. As Beechler & Woodward (2009) and Groysberg (2006) suggest, the skills and experience that stars bring into an organization are more likely to transfer effectively when the new environment is similar to the old one, when the values are shared, and when cultural fit is taken into account.

Finally, firms looking for future potential might search for people that show promise of occupying an important position in the company in the long run. In this case the selection process needs to observe a set of competencies in the candidates. These competencies provide the companies a mechanism for filtering the candidates. Here are some of the selection methods that might help an organization finding the most talented people to meet its needs.

3.2.2.1 Interviews

Interviews are widely used and, when used properly, can be a reliable selection method. Conducting an interview properly means that the focus of the interview should change depending on what the recruiter would like to explore. However, this is something many interviewers do not take into account and, consequently, the content of the interview often becomes irrelevant. Indeed, it is astonishing how many firms do not bother to take this step more seriously when hiring.

If the focus of the interview is to explore a candidate's experience, then a behavioral interview is appropriate. Bowers & Kleiner (2005, p. 107) define a behavioral interview as 'the systematic use of job-related, open-ended questions to help measure a candidate's skills for a particular job'. That is, candidates are asked to provide examples that demonstrate the skills they have used. The aim of the interview is to predict what the candidate would do if he or she was working in a specific role at the firm. Such an interview is completely different from asking hypothetical questions that can only be addressed with hypothetical answers.

Clifford et al. (2006) point out that the use of behavioral interviews almost triples the correlation between traditional interviews and job success. However, for a behavioral interview to be successful, there must be a strong correlation between the questions to be asked and the skills to be probed. Organizations conducting behavioral interviews should therefore carefully consider which questions they are going to ask and what skills they believe are the most important for a particular job. For instance, if the recruiter wants to test a candidate's ability to confront adversity, it may ask, 'Tell me when you have failed at your job/task/objective'. If the recruiter wants to ascertain the analytical ability of the candidate, it could try, for example, 'Tell me about the information you used to analyze a critical decision' or 'Do you use statistics or any numerical methodology to inform your decision-making process? Can you give me examples?' or 'What are the steps you followed in making your decision? Describe those steps.' Do not ask yes-no questions such as, 'Are you creative?', where the obvious answer is yes. Rather, to probe such a skill the recruiter may try to take the negative side of it and ask: 'Tell me about a time when being creative was a drawback to your work.'

By using a behavioral interview, organizations can avoid making the mistake of dismissing talented people before they have even started the interview because the interviewer may not like the look of the interviewee. That is, this interview technique helps the interviewer avoid making decisions about the candidate based upon nothing more than gut feeling.

In addition to assessing candidates' skills, interviews can be used to assess candidates' competencies and potential. In this case, it is critical to have a clear list of competencies to be assessed when conducting the interview (Grigoryev, 2006). Going into detail about a candidate's professional background, education, and types of organizations in which the candidate has worked might help the recruiter understand whether the candidate fits the organization. Group interviews can also be a good way to lead interviewers towards the right hiring decision.

Although interviews tend to be a reliable selection method when conducted properly, it is advisable to combine different methods. In particular, using various methods can allow a company to verify or challenge the conclusions drawn from an interview, thereby helping ensure that the organization brings the right talent on board.

Off the record

Reshaping the map of competencies in order to hire the best people

What are the best competencies to use to assess talent? Nobody knows but everybody has a list of desirable competencies. However, in most cases, such lists are useless. The reason is that most firms spend a lot of money on consultants, workshops, and pilot studies to discover the core attributes of the

(Continued)

organization. As a result, the core competencies that are supposed to be a source of competitive advantage are just the same set of core competencies used by other firms, albeit with slightly different names. Indeed, a study of multinationals (Figueiredo & Hatum, 2004) that mapped the competencies of the firms analyzed found that most of the competencies were similar. Customer orientation, service orientation, flexibility, proactive attitude, and analytical thinking, among other attributes, were commonly listed at the sample firms.

At the end of the day the question to ask is whether a firm's list of core competencies helps the firm to hire and develop its best talent. Theoretically, a firm's core competencies should make it possible for the organization to differentiate itself from its competitors. We argue that in today's talent mess era, exacerbated by a huge international financial crisis, the list of competencies currently used is unable to help companies meet this objective. Companies should thus reassess their list of competencies to make sure that it works to help them hire talented people who will meet the firm's needs. For example, companies need to further explore employees' ability to manage in a complex context, the extent of their business and personal agility, and their ability to manage change, rather than their ability to take the initiative, innovate or be proactive. In summary, firms need to identify those competencies that can allow them to differentiate themselves, and those competencies should then be used to improve the hiring process such that talent can be identified, hired, and make a difference in the organization.

3.2.2.2 Assessment centers

To assess a candidate's organizational fit or potential, the firm might turn to an assessment center. Assessment centers are not a method per *se*. Rather, they involve the use of a combination of methods that together reveal a candidate's attitudes, potential, and even competencies. Clifford et al. (2006) suggest that work samples are proven predictors of success and can be simple to arrange and implement. The assessments can also be a good way to predict how one might behave in a group. To benefit from using assessment centers, the company generally needs to have a clear idea of what it is looking for in an individual. Southwest Airlines, for example, uses various methods in its assessments with one simple objective: find the best people with the best attitude who will be a good fit with Southwest's culture. Hiring for attitude is the primary aim of the People Department (Human Resources).

Herb Kelleher, the founder of the firm, used to say: 'We look for attitudes; people with a sense of humor who don't take themselves too seriously. We'll train you on whatever it is you have to do, but the one thing Southwest cannot change in people is inherent attitudes' (Freiberg & Freiberg, 1998, p. 67). To determine whether candidates have the Southwest spirit, customers are sometimes involved in interviews for new flight attendants. Similarly, pilots are often involved in interviews for new pilots. Applicants also go through an array of different activities, which might include drawing pictures (Southwest prefers to hire those who draw outside the lines) or making a presentation about the candidate's life and experience.[25]

At *Cirque du Soleil*, the selection process entails identifying individuals who are not only talented, but also a good fit for the company's multicultural and hardworking environment. Once recruited, candidates are brought to Montreal, where *Cirque du Soleil's* headquarters is located. There they will be trained in their artistic speciality, but at the same time, Cirque tests the artistes' core values. In particular, Cirque evaluates candidates' ability to work in a team, willingness to take artistic risks, generosity towards the spectator, and ability to solve creative problems (Heward & Bacon, 2006). Once the company is assured that the candidate will fit the firm, the candidate receives an offer.[26]

Best practices at a glance

Like in the theatre: assessment center based on casting at Faena Hotel+Universe

The Faena Hotel+Universe (http://www.faenahotelanduniverse.com), designed by the much sought-after designer Phillipe Starck, is located in Buenos Aires, Argentina. The exuberance of the hotel attracted the attention of not only specialized magazines, but also the prestigious *Financial Times*.[27] The hotel has no reception. Each guest is assigned to an Experience Manager who makes sure that the guest will have the best stay possible, indulging and pampering the guest as necessary. Such high levels of customer service required a departure from the usual hiring process. Indeed, as the hotel's General Manager observed, 'In the hotel industry, you try to find people with experience in the same sector. We craved something completely different. We have identified our aim [to be] "passion". It is of the utmost importance [that] our staff be the most gracious host or hostess...To find these passionate people we needed a different approach towards the

(Continued)

selection process'.[28] The hotel began by hiring a Casting Manager, who was an actress, to oversee the selection process. The Training Manager explained, 'The General Manager has imagined this hotel as a theatre where once you are on the stage it is impossible to go backwards. We wanted passionate people; we were later in charge of training them.'[29] To identify which applicants had the desired passion, candidates were interviewed and then asked to participate in an innovative role-play exercise where actors played the part of the guest. These groups of actors performed diverse scenarios and the applicants had to devise and implement solutions to the challenges presented.

The results were highly positive. As the General Manager pointed out, 'With this [selection] process we were able to put people in the best places for them and for the organization. Besides, we were also able to reduce the normal turnover experienced by other competitors.'[30]

3.2.2.3 Other methods frequently used

Testing can complement an interview or assessment center. However, the market is flooded by tests. *Psychometric tests*, as Davis et al. (2007) state, cover a variety of assessment techniques. For example, they seek to determine an individual's expected or future behavior in terms of aptitude, attitude and personality. Aptitude or ability tests measure different aspects of critical reasoning (verbal, logical, abstraction capability, among others). Interests and values are usually assessed by means of attitude tests. In contrast, personality assessments, which are very popular indeed, try to find the stable elements of one's personality. These tests are based on categories that aim to identify a personality preference. The Myers Briggs Type Indicators (MBTI) is a well-known personality test. The personality types identified by the MBTI allow firms to place individuals according to one of the 16 preferred styles. Psychometric testing can then allow the firm to assess a candidate's cognitive abilities or personality traits.

References can also be important if the future employer takes them seriously. In speaking with referees, recruiters should avoid asking general questions that would naturally lead to oversimplified answers. In addition, while the employee may suggest a couple of names as referees, a good referral process will entail searching for neutral opinions on the candidate's professional background and behavior.

To recap, the selection process can be powerful as it has the ability to shape and mould the organization (Wilk & Capelli, 2003). The methods used in a company's selection process should thus be the result of deep analysis as to what attributes the company is looking for in its employees. This implies that the selection process should avoid following methodological fads and fashion, but instead should use those methods or practices that will enable the company to hire the talent it requires. If a given method does not offer the organization a good hiring result, then it should not be used further. Note the importance of not relying on one method only. A candidate might impress an interviewer but may fail a different assessment. It is therefore important to employ various types of assessment to get a clear picture of a candidate's strengths and ability to fit the corporate culture, leading in turn to a better result when hiring. We are highlighting the importance of combining the different methods analysed to get a better result when hiring. Furthermore, combining methods in the selection process as Philbrick et al. (1999) confirm, increases the validity of the whole process. Table 3.1 summarizes how some of the methods discussed above can be applied to address different company needs and increase the validity of the process.

As Table 3.1 illustrates, a focus on finding experienced talent would ideally involve the use of behavioral interviews. However, by also

TABLE 3.1 **Best methods to find the best people**

Methods Focus	First choice	Second choice	Third choice
Focus on experience	Behavioral interview	Cognitive testing (or ability, if technical knowledge is required)	References
Focus on attitude and fit	Individual and group interviews	References	Psychometric testing (cognitive/personality)
Focus on potential	Assessment center	Individual and group interviews	Cognitive testing

conducting cognitive testing and talking with referees, the company can confirm the claimed ability and experience of the candidate. If the focus is instead on attitude, individual and group interviews may help the company gauge the candidate's fit. However, as before, references and psychometric testing can help corroborate what the company learns in the interviews about the candidate's attitude. Finally, a focus on potential should involve the use of assessment centers, which can reveal candidates' competencies. However, interviews and cognitive testing can also be used to validate the results of the assessment centers.

This chapter has focused on attraction, that is, on how a company's recruiting and selection processes can be used to identify and ultimately hire the best possible talent for the company. However, attracting good people to a company is just the beginning of a process that should be seen as a continuum in which everything the company does to hire and retain talent takes into account the impact of its messages and actions on employees' expectations. The firm should seek to communicate realistic expectations that it is able to fulfil, and it should take into account the way the attraction processes connect with development and retention. Development and retention are discussed in the following chapters. Before turning to these topics, this chapter concludes with a 'Case in point' which illustrates one leading firm's tightly integrated staffing practices and aligns them towards the business strategy.

CASE IN POINT: L'ORÉAL

L'ORÉAL®

L'Oréal: staffing as a business strategy

Founded 100 years ago, L'Oréal is a leading developer, manufacturer, and distributor of cosmetics, hair care products, and fragrances worldwide. In 2009, the company owned 23 global brands, generated 17 billion euros in sales, and employed more than 67,000 staff in its different businesses spread across 130 countries.[31] The group's major global brands allow L'Oréal to provide consumers with a portfolio of products with diverse cultural origins that satisfy tastes all around the world. Some of L'Oréal's major brands are as follows:

- Professional products: L'Oréal, Kérastase, Matrix, Mizani, Pureology, Redken
- Consumer products: Garnier, L'Oréal Paris, Maybelline, SoftSheen-Carson
- Luxury products: Biotherm, Cacharel, Diesel, Giorgio Armani, Guy Laroche, Helena Rubinstein, Kiehl's, Lancome, Paloma Picasso, Ralph Lauren, Shu Uemura, Viktor & Rolf, YSL Beauté
- Active cosmetics: Dermablend, Innéov, La Roche-Posay, Sanoflore, SkinCeuticals, Vichy
- The Body Shop: Acquired by L'Oréal in 2006, the firm founded by Anita Roddick allows L'Oréal to penetrate a market of naturally inspired cosmetics.

The company's slogan 'to build beauty, we need talent' conveys the strategic importance of staffing to the firm. Indeed, as the Executive Vice President of Human Resources, observes, 'The fundamental challenge is to be able to engender the next generation of people who will produce working tenures in our company. And that, because we are now on a global scale, is complex. We need to attract the best professionals who are passionate about this business.'[32]

To meet its staffing objective L'Oréal has developed a staffing model with six recruitment dimensions that helps the firm ensure a successful hiring outcome. The different dimensions of the staffing model, which is known as 'the wheel', are presented in Figure 3.4.[33]

The first dimension in L'Oréal's staffing model focuses on attracting candidates. In an effort to attract as many good candidates

6 recruitment dimensions:

✓ Attracting the candidates

✓ Sourcing them actively

✓ Select the best candidates

✓ Being sure of a solid integration

✓ Build strong relationships, internally and externally

✓ Anticipate changes

FIGURE 3.4 **L'Oréal's staffing model**

    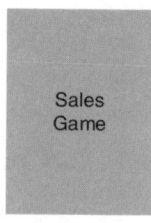

General business : started 2000 126 *countries*	Marketing: started 1993 39 *countries*	R&D : started 2007 *France* + 3	Engineering : started 2001 11 *countries*	Sales : tested 2008 *France*

FIGURE 3.5 **Games portfolio at L'Oréal**

as possible, the company uses five different business games (see Figure 3.5):[34] e-strat (for business, launched in 2000 and L'Oréal's most widely known game); Brandstorm (for marketing, 1993); Ingenius (for engineers, 2001); Innovation Lab (for researchers, 2007); and Sales (for sales specialists, tested during 2008). The International Co-ordinator for Corporate Communication explains: 'Business games were helpful to enable us to access the universities and business schools. They also boosted our image as a professional company in which people were able to develop a professional career.'[35]

The next dimension of the model focuses on actively sourcing new employees. At L'Oréal, the belief is that great talent is hard to find and attract, and thus when such talent surfaces the organization must be able to find a place for them. For instance, the International Recruitment Development Director, observes that, 'it is important to have a pool of talent to respond quickly to the business' needs. Our "pepinière" aims at that, at being ready whenever the organization needs a person.'[36] The Recruitment Manager for Cosmetics, agrees: 'A key [aim] for us is to find talent wherever it is. I am looking for individual skills. We, as recruiters, have the freedom to hire someone because we think he or she is the right person for the company. We do not recruit for a position, we recruit for the group. If we think he or she is great, we hire them.'[37]

The third dimension of the model focuses on using multiple selection methods to choose the right candidates. L'Oréal's flagship games are an important part of this dimension. These games are supported by active recruiting at university campuses. Moreover, e-recruiting is a critical part of L'Oréal's selection process. Through L'Oréal's HR Trends

Observatory, for instance, the company was able to further explore and innovate its recruitment process by analyzing the possibilities internet and e-recruiting offered. In addition, the company posts jobs and recruiting videos on communication channels such as YouTube, Facebook, Hi5, and LinkedIn. The diversity of recruitment tools used is a consequence of the various profiles, products, and businesses the company has – the idea of diversity is rooted in the foundation of the company: 'We have a strong diversity criteria in handling our business and we want to make sure that we are attracting a whole range of different people...we have to transmit the passion, identify the people, create opportunity, and be able to do that across the globe.'[38] Figure 3.6[39] shows L'Oréal's view of the contributors and goals of diversity.

While active sourcing and a wide range of selection methods can guarantee that the company attracts and recruits a diversity of people, this is not the end of the staffing process. The fourth and fifth dimensions of L'Oréal's staffing model relate to integration and building relationships. The International Recruitment Development Director, explains: 'Once we have people on board we need them to have a smooth process of immersion in the company's culture, way of doing, and values. This is the aim of our FIT programme.'[40] FIT (Follow-up and Integration Track) is a two-year personalized integration program

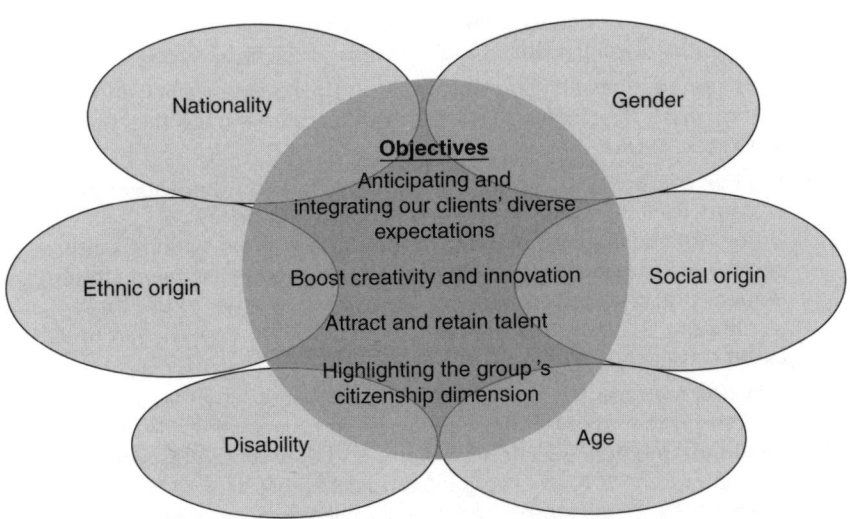

FIGURE 3.6 **Diversity at L'Oréal**

that allows each new employee to learn how the company works. This program also serves to create a sense of belonging, inspire loyalty, and help employees anticipate career development opportunities. Finally, it aims to integrate diverse profiles to enrich the firm's culture.

FIT starts with a warm welcome, followed by an introduction to the field and products. The new recruit then receives training and on-the-job learning supported by line managers and human resources. The new recruit also participates in round-table discussions and personalized meetings. The program thus involves managers, human resource teams, and the employee.[41] 'Attracting and recruiting talent is one side of the coin. The other side is integration. We recruit with the idea of retaining. That is why our staffing process is so successful and effective.'[42]

The final dimension of L'Oréal's staffing model relates to anticipating changes. The company is constantly deepening its understanding of new trends in the market. Through the Trends Observatory and the experience the company acquires through the simulations, L'Oréal is able to build a staffing process based on sophisticated technology that meets the strategic needs of the business.

CHAPTER HIGHLIGHTS

❖ Talent and talent management should seek to deliver the organizational competencies that the firm needs to be successful.

❖ Attraction requires thinking deeply about the company's EVP and staffing processes. Staffing includes both recruitment and selection processes.

❖ The EVP comprises the firm's organizational features that allow it to promote itself outwardly and generate loyalty internally. Organizational features included in the EVP are: organizational culture; people; work characteristics; and rewards. A good recruitment strategy requires organizations to segment the market, in order to use those recruitment channels that are best suited to attract a specific group of target candidates.

❖ Selection methods may vary depending on whether the hiring objective is to find potential, experience, or organizational fit. Firms should use multiple selection methods, and they should tailor their selection methods to the group of candidates they seek to hire. Among the methods to be explored are behavioral interviews, assessment centers, testing, and references.

VERY IMPORTANT QUESTIONS

- Has your company aligned its talent with the organizational capabilities needed to compete and succeed?
- Has your organization worked on a realistic and convincing EVP?
- Has your company explored and analyzed the organizational features of the EVP, namely, organizational culture, people, work characteristics, and rewards?
- Has your company designed different recruitment approaches for the different generations?
- Is your firm targeting different segments using different recruitment channels?
- Are the selection processes aligned with the organization's needs?
- Is the selection process used actually attracting the best candidates?

4

TALENT MANAGEMENT STEP 2: BROADENING THE SCOPE OF DEVELOPMENT

As a result of the organization's recruiting and selection efforts, the company now has new people on board, in addition to employees who have been with the company for a long time. A sound talent management strategy must include processes for blending all these people together to form a harmonious workforce. In addition, the organization needs to have a development strategy, so that talent is ready to meet the company's changing needs. This chapter explores the development of a firm's talent management strategy.

The next generation talent management has resulted in the outright overturn of several paradigms that were once widely accepted among companies with regard to their employees' development. For example, whereas firms formerly sought to determine whether to raise people from within or hire them from the employment market, in today's context it is important to do both. Similarly, it is no longer useful to determine whether the company should focus on succession planning (through a suitable and organized pipeline) or the creation of talent pools; rather, companies should now do both.

Let's consider the question of whether to raise talent from within or to hire people from the employment market, that is, whether to 'make or buy' (Capelli, 2008). Both activities are critical for firms in the current talent context. The idea of 'making' talent comes from an era in which people trusted their organizations and developed their careers with them, believing they would climb the corporate ladder and stay with the same company until they retired. Companies also believed in this commitment and were willing to support their employees by every possible means. After the Second World War, the booming economy and market stability together helped reinforce these ideas. Hence, companies developed succession plans to fit the hierarchical structures that were in use at the time, and that in some cases are still in use. The succession pipeline was nurtured starting at the bottom of the pyramid to make sure that, after a long period of development and preparation, young professionals ultimately became strong managers.

General Electric (GE) is a prime example of an organization that has used a develop-and-promote-from-within approach (Capelli, 2008b), as 85% to 90% of its top 600 leaders are all former employees. However, it is also true that many of GE's top executives leave the firm to take leadership positions at other major companies.[1] This raises the question as to whether a rigid system such as this one is truly the right system to use, especially in an era characterized by market turmoil, overlapping generations, and the presence of a new generation that views job-hopping to be the swiftest way forward.

In a context that is highly volatile and in which skills are rendered outdated at speeds never seen before, rising from within should also be complemented with external hiring, so that the company is able to moderate the effects of market swings or of people leaving to try new jobs and challenges elsewhere. Thus, 'make or buy' is now 'make and buy'. Put differently, these two options no longer share an either/or relationship, but a complementary relationship. This complementarity influences the relevance of the other traditional paradigm that was presented at the beginning of this chapter, namely, whether an organization should focus on succession planning or create talent pools.

Succession planning is the practice of identifying individuals who can fill specific leadership roles in the future. A talent pool, in contrast, is created when organizations identify a 'pool' or group of individuals to develop for a specific job, rather than specific successors to replace a given leader (Gay & Sims, 2006, p. 45). The creation of talent pools is a critical managerial decision. Boudreau & Ramstad (2005) state that improving the quality and availability of talent pools is not only critical but also a decision with a huge impact on the talent strategy of the company ('talentship' for the authors). The old paradigm established the importance of developing a succession pipeline to guarantee the existence of a successor when needed. However, while the use of succession pipelines continues to be important when taking a long-term perspective on careers in one's own company, the arrival of a generation of employees who value job-hopping over long-term employment raises the question of how to ensure a stable succession plan. Put differently, companies that continue to focus largely on succession planning are likely to face a leak in their pipeline as 'successors' leave the company to pursue other opportunities elsewhere. This can be particularly problematic when the candidate successor leaves the company just when the company is nearly ready to promote that person to replace an outgoing leader, as the years of investment in that individual simply slip away. Thus, in the next generation talent management era, not only is the use of succession planning not enough, but it can also be down-right dangerous if it is the only system that a company employs to develop its staff. A broader outlook is therefore needed to confront the current market's complexity.

In particular, the use of talent pools can complement the more traditional system of choosing a candidate successor that is groomed to thrive in a certain position. A talent pool allows an organization to fill the pool with first-rate professionals who have the potential to occupy positions as they become available. Organizations that make use of talent pools enjoy a tremendous advantage over competitors that limit themselves to standard succession plans. First, companies that use talent pools enjoy greater flexibility stemming from the fact that pools are broader than normal pipelines – companies that use talent pools are not limited to the one candidate chosen to succeed an outgoing manager, but rather can choose from many potential candidates as positions become available. Second, companies that use talent pools can easily supply a candidate for a position, and thus are less exposed to candidate successors leaving the company and generating the problem of having to identify a new successor and prepare him or her for the job. Third, for some firms, identifying specific successors is quite difficult, if not impossible, because some potential successors leave the organization, which raises questions about the value of investing heavily in specific candidate successors.

To summarize, similar to the question of whether to hire from inside the company or outside the company, the question of whether to use succession planning or create talent pools is no longer relevant; these practices are complements and, thus, both should be used. Some organizations, for example, may carry out a position vacancy risk analysis and create a succession plan for high-risk positions, while also generating talent pools for other positions.

What kinds of 'pools' might an organization create? One company may decide to create a talent pool to fill top financial positions in a multinational company or a talent pool of high potential individuals. Still other firms may create talent pools that correspond to different business units or functional areas, or talent pools for, say, project managers (Heinen & O'Neill, 2004).

Vacancy risk analysis, in contrast, might be of great use if done properly, taking into consideration that each position's risk has two components: the degree of difficulty the organization faces in replacing a person in a particular position and the value added of the position to the firm's effect in the market. Some analyses tend to focus more on the latter, leaving replacement-difficulty issues aside. Figure 4.1 illustrates the interaction between the two vacancy risk factors.

Similar matrices have been proposed previously by Zuboff (1988) and more recently by Lewis & Heckman (2006). In Figure 4.1, there are four quadrants. Positions that present the greatest vacancy risk to the organization are located in the top right of the matrix. More specifically, this quadrant captures high value-added positions that have an important impact in the market, are critical to the organization, and that are also difficult to fill in the labor market. Such positions might include top management jobs that have a strategic role in the company. The lower right quadrants capture positions that are difficult to fill but that have little value added in terms of market impact. These positions might include highly qualified experts that have no direct

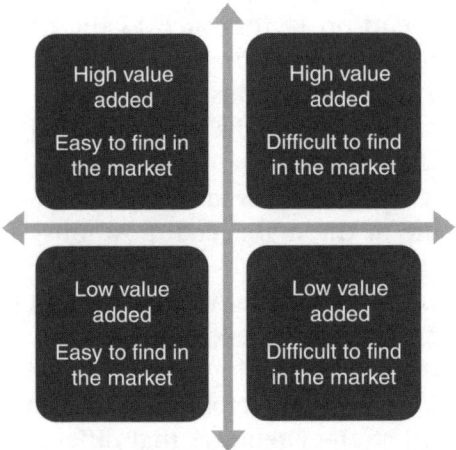

FIGURE 4.1 **Risk of position vacancy**

impact on customers. Positions that are easy to fill and that have a high market impact are located in the top left quadrant. These positions should be differentiated so that they become a competitive advantage to the organization. Finally, positions in the lower left part of the matrix are those that have little value added in terms of contribution and are easy to fill. Such positions are not of great concern in terms of vacancy risk analysis.

An interesting aspect of this methodology is the fact that an organization can determine whether all of its best players are in one quadrant or another. A company that finds that most of its talented individuals are difficult to replace (high value added) would learn that it faces a high degree of human capital and, in turn, operational risk, and hence can work toward diversifying its talent mix such that fewer high talent individuals are in this one quadrant.

In a similar fashion, Collings & Mellahi (2009) argue that strategic talent management includes the identification of pivotal talent positions. Indeed, the authors suggest that such identification should be the first step in any strategic talent management system. Pivotal positions are those that have the potential to differentially influence the firm's competitive advantage (Collings & Mellahi, 2009, p. 307). In this context the authors emphasize the importance of the position, not the individual employee. They therefore focus on 'A positions' rather than 'A players'.

Turning back to the discussion on which positions should ultimately be sourced via a succession plan versus a talent pool, this decision should depend on factors such as the organization's needs, the industry the firm competes in, and the complexity of the positions within the firm and the industry. A talent pool strategy can be useful when there is a large managerial population and the career ladder is volatile. In contrast, a clear succession plan may be preferred when managerial positions are few, and due to the industry's special features some of the managerial positions are critical (Barner, 2006).

In broadening the scope of the organizational talent base, a company should consider employee development as an integral part of the talent management process. Employee development involves gathering different population targets across the organization. Furthermore, a broad development strategy requires that different methods be used to develop different individuals within the organization. These issues are discussed in the following sections.

Best practices at a glance

Talent pools for future success

Puig is a family owned fragrance, cosmetics, and fashion firm from Barcelona, Spain. With more than a billion euros of net revenues and 3500 employees, Puig owns prestigious perfume brands such as Paco Rabanne, Carolina Herrera, and Nina Ricci, among others. The firm also commercializes a portfolio of important designer brands such as Adolfo Domínguez, Prada, Massimo Dutti, and Mango.[2]

By 2005, less than 10% of Puig's middle and senior managers had been recruited from outside the company.[3] Puig therefore needed to strengthen the development of its executives. To do so, the company created different talent pools throughout the organization. The Chief of Human Resources and Chief Legal Officer explains: 'We called our project Jano, because Jano is a god with two faces. One is young, looking toward the future, but we never forget the other face, the older one, which is our feeling towards the past.'[4] The firm's history is important to Puig. Being a family organization, the company wants to attract talented people but also wants to take care to ensure that new recruits will fit the organization's culture. But to achieve the company's strategic vision for the future, which includes expanding into new markets, the company wants to ensure that hiring decisions are aligned with the firm's goals. Thus, in creating the organization's talent pools, the definition of talent depends on the position's role in Puig's strategy. Put differently, there is no one definition for talent, but rather the characterization of talent is attached to the pools the firm created.

The creation of talent pools took into consideration both the current situation and the anticipated challenges of the company. 'We organized three different profiles that became three talent pools: the fast-trackers, who are the leaders for the future; the specialists, who are good at innovating; and the unsung heroes, who excel and are very efficient in processes.'[5]

These three talent pools were designed in a way that made the profile, priorities, and challenges of each group clear. As an example, fast-trackers include those people considered high potentials, stars or hidden stars. Their profile contains a mix of performance and leadership competencies rated at the highest levels. Among the priorities for this pool, development in terms of both hierarchical and experiential growth is deemed critical, as are motivation and retention. The challenge for this group focuses mainly on providing individuals with assignments to stretch their competencies.

(Continued)

Creating and managing talent pools requires a huge amount of involvement of managers throughout the organization. 'You need involvement from the local HR people, regional HR managers, and line managers. They know who the talents are. Identifying people for talent pools is a critical requirement and you need everybody's support.'[6]

4.1 TARGETING TALENT FOR DEVELOPMENT

Who should the organization develop? To address this question, one should keep in mind that development is different from training. Training focuses on a specific task that the individual will perform in the short term, whereas development focuses on preparing the individual to deal with more complex matters in the future. Development focuses on the long term. Organizations should target for development those talents that will be critical for its future success. This implies that to determine who should be developed, the firm should consider its future business needs.

Common targets for development include individuals who are entrenched in the leadership pipeline, individuals with high potential, strong performers, and critical talent, among others. Byham et al. (2002, p. 61) define high potentials as those who are likely to be able to advance at least two or three levels within the organization. Here, high potentials are defined as those individuals with the ability to grow and manage more complex matters in the future. Performance is not set aside; on the contrary, performance is one way of identifying people you may think have potential. But to measure performance it is necessary to look back to the past. Strong performers (at any level of the organization) are usually great individual contributors with a good track record; their contributions often have a large impact on the organization's results, although they are not always as valued as they should be. Critical talent refers to experts or specialists; a group that can have a large influence on the results of the company in the future. For example, an expert might be a geologist working at an oil company. Few people in the labor market have such expertise, but the geologist's role is vital to the company's future performance. The organization can apply many methods to identify various talents to be targeted for development. However, regardless of the method used, two criteria should drive the decision of who to develop: strong past performance and strong future potential.

In looking at an individual's past performance, an organization should consider not only the individual's performance appraisal, but also the behavioral patterns that helped the individual to achieve his or her results. A candidate needs to get results (the 'what' question) but, at the same time, the way the performance objectives have been achieved is important (the 'how' question). A closer examination of the competencies defined by the company or the values the firm is supporting might help get a better insight of the candidate's real performance.

One company that considers results and behaviors (or leadership behaviors) when assessing managers is British American Tobacco (BAT), the international tobacco group. The Global Leadership and Talent Development Manager of BAT explains: 'Many firms have this leadership capability in their set of competencies, but the big question is how do you embed this in your business. Most companies talk about it but they don't really measure it. At BAT this is critical.'[7] The reason an individual's behavior or leadership is important is that strong past performance may not necessarily lead to strong future performance if the behaviors used to achieve the results are not aligned with the corporate culture.

To illustrate this point, Figure 4.2 presents a matrix that plots 'what' results are delivered (great vs. bad) against 'how' these results are delivered (again, great vs. bad).

As Figure 4.2 illustrates, just looking at 'what' a person has achieved may cause problems for a company. Focusing first on an organization's strong performers, who presumably are the most likely targets for development, Figure 4.2 shows that there are two types of strong performers: on the one hand, a star, and on the other, an organizational beast. Both are good performers, but the star also knows how to deal with people, thereby not harming the organization in the process of producing results. Meanwhile, the organizational beast may cause suffering with his or her unbearable behavior or unstable temperament and his or her 'abrasive personality' (Levison, 1978). Thus, the biggest difference between these two groups stems from 'how' they achieve their results. Turning to the poor performers, those with poor attitudes should be expelled from the company before they undermine overall organizational performance. Those that are 'nice but incompetent', in contrast, display useful behaviors that are aligned with the organizational culture but simply are not performing well. These people should

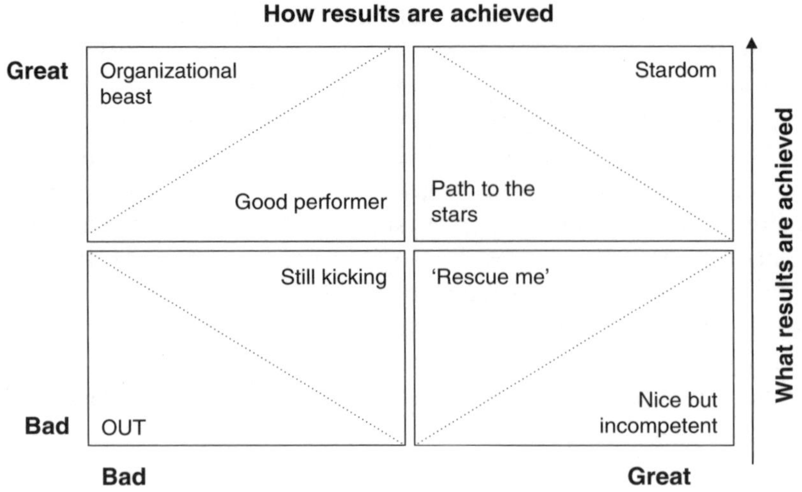

How results are achieved

FIGURE 4.2 **Performance and competencies: what and how results are achieved**

be given an opportunity to demonstrate their managerial quality in terms of performance, perhaps by moving them to another area.

To summarize, the matrix in Figure 4.2 shows how analyzing the interaction between what results are delivered and how they are delivered can help the company identify individuals to target for development. What is the best way to determine in which of the matrix categories an individual belongs? This will depend on the type of performance appraisal used by the firm: top-down, self-assessment, peer evaluation, force distribution curve, or a combination of methods. However, whatever method is used, it should include a broad analysis of an individual's performance and behaviors so that those persons targeted for development are those who are most likely to display both positive results and exceptional interpersonal skills in the future.

Off the record

Too many 'stars' can blow things apart

On one of the first pages of the book entitled *The War for Talent* is this quote: 'The only thing that differentiates Enron from our competitors is our people, our talent'. The quote continues, 'The whole battle going forward will be for talent. In fact, it has been that way for the last decade. Some people just didn't notice it' (Michaels et al., 2001, p. 2). Interestingly, this quote comes from Kenneth Lay, former Chairman of Enron. During the 1990s Enron hired a large number of newly minted MBA students, and the company rewarded top performers extremely well. Enron was a place where stars did whatever they wanted and were promoted regardless of their seniority or experience.[8]

However, Enron's culture of rewarding exceptional performers was blind to the importance of building real stars rather than selfish organizational beasts that have only one thing in mind: their own benefit. The importance Enron gave to individual talent resulted in lack of alignment with the firm's values, strategies, and people. Eventually, Enron went bankrupt, leaving us with a good example of what companies should not do when managing talent at their organizations.

Recall that strong past performance is one of two criteria to use in identifying talent to develop; the other criterion is strong future potential. However, finding high potential people can be tricky. The reason is that a high current or past performer may not be a high future-potential individual, although high potentials generally tend to be good performers. To discover high potentials an organization should focus on a person's advancement potential. Some firms view advancement potential as the potential to move to the next level within two years. Others may define advancement potential as the potential to advance two levels within the next five years. Obviously, advancements require that individuals manage more complex tasks as they move from one level to the next. The level that a person is expected to be able to reach within the organization is indicative of their expected ability to cope with each new task given them.

The ability to manage increasing complexity is related to another factor that can help an organization discern potential: the ability to learn. High potential people are natural learners. Lombardo & Eichinger (2000) characterize high potential people as high learners. These individuals are keen to innovate, take risks, and change. All of these attributes are consequences of their learning capability.

When searching to identify high potential candidates, the company's values should be taken into account. The reason is that the investment in development is huge, and thus firms need to be sure they identify targets that share the organization's values and cultural sensibility, as otherwise the individual may leave the company and render the investment a loss. Figure 4.3 depicts the basic elements to look for to discover high potentials.

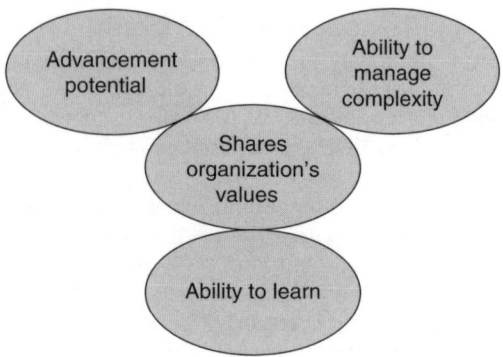

FIGURE 4.3 **Discovering potential**

To distinguish 'high potentials' from 'high performers', Royal Mail uses predictive differentiators, or lead indicators, that provide an index of one's capacity for further growth. These differentiators are based on main agilities such as strategic agility, emotional agility, and learning agility.[9] Royal Mail then breaks these categories down into sub-categories such as, 'Do people focus on the big picture? Are they able to cope with commercial complexity?'[10] These differentiators work to distinguish high potentials.

The potential assessment should be conducted separately from the performance assessment so that those involved in the process are less likely to find the same results as those involved with the performance assessment. Who should be involved in the potential evaluation depends on the assessment process used. Some firms prefer that only the upper echelon of the corporation be involved in the potential evaluation. Other firms may use a nomination process. It is worth pointing out that the broader the talent assessment process is (i.e., the larger the number of high potential categories, the larger number of talent pools), the more leaders will need to be included in the assessment process. For example, when the talent assessment is restricted to one group (successors, a specific group of high potentials), fewer people may be needed to participate (e.g., top team). In any case, the more inclusive the assessment process is, the more widely the talent mindset (Michaels et al., 2001) will be spread through the organization.

With the separate potential and performance assessments, leaders are ready to use the results to determine who to target for development. A potential-performance matrix can facilitate this process. Using the animal world as a metaphor, we might build a matrix such as that

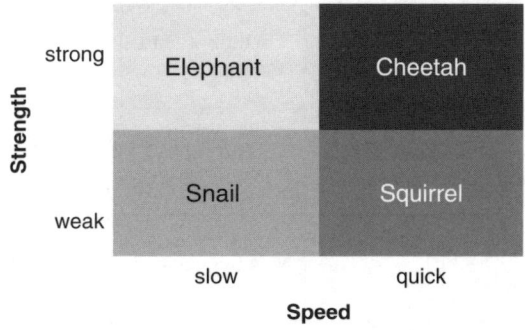

FIGURE 4.4 **Performance and potential matrix: a metaphor**

in Figure 4.4 in which performance and potential are represented by strength and speed, respectively. In this matrix there are four types of animals, namely, cheetahs, snails, elephants, and squirrels. Cheetahs are among the fastest and strongest land animals on Earth. Snails are the polar opposite, being among the slowest and weakest animals in nature. Elephants bear the crown for strength but are rather slow, whereas squirrels have little strength but can move very quickly. If these four animals were to be put into a shared space (the organization), the type with the greatest future prospects would be the cheetah. In contrast, snails would fare the worst. Analogously, employees that have the greatest expected potential and performance are most likely to contribute to the firm's future success, whereas those that have poor expected potential and performance are least likely to contribute.

Of course, the matrix in Figure 4.4 may be too simple to capture the results of a firm's potential and performance assessments. In that case one can extend the model to allow for intermediate categories in which to place people (see Figure 4.5).

To summarize, using a matrix such as those presented in Figures 4.4 or 4.5 can help organizations distinguish who is who among their associates. In turn, firms will be able to determine who to target for development. Moreover, once talent has been identified, a firm can adopt measures to decrease the chance of losing this talent.

Sometimes the problem for a company is not how to discover and find a category for each person, but how to find the best way to develop its people in order to reach its best potential. Lastminute.com is an

	Poor	Good	Strong
Strong	Conundrum	On their way to the top	Stars
Good	Just a soldier	Average	On their way to the top
Poor	Out	Nice but useless	Conundrum

Performance (vertical axis)

Potential (horizontal axis): Poor, Good, Strong

FIGURE 4.5 **Performance and potential matrix: an extended model**

example of a company that uses the nine-grid matrix tool. The company considers this methodology critical to being able to spot high potentials as well as short- and long-term successors. However, to go from the matrix to clear development decisions, the company digs more deeply into each level of the matrix. The Learning and Development Manager explains: 'If we talk about high potential people we need to ask ourselves, are they still high potentials? Are we following the actions put in place? What are we going to do this year? The matrix is part of a cascade process in which every year we calibrate people'.[11]

Best practices at a glance

Development and performance at Pfizer

Pfizer is the world's largest research-based biomedical and pharmaceutical company. The firm is a global leader in both research and development (R&D), with US$48.3 bn revenues in 2008 and US$7.9 bn of R&D investment.[12]

The company engaged in a series of mergers and acquisitions during the 1990s and early 2000s, and has recently announced the acquisition of another laboratory: Wyeth. The combined company will create one of the most diversified companies in the global healthcare industry and the largest laboratory in the world.

As a result of this growth, the company has been transforming its approach to human resources. One of the processes being changed is performance management. The Performance Management Leader explains: 'One of the dangers of performance management is when people feel that it doesn't make sense or it doesn't have an impact on their work, career development, and engagement. Another mistake is when it is taken as a tool and not as a process.'[13] Before, performance management at Pfizer was regarded as a tool that aimed largely at appraisal assessment, and human resources was its owner–administrator.

Today, performance management is regarded as a process and the responsibility is shared by colleagues, leaders, and managers alike: 'Colleagues and leaders are the owners of the process. They have to define and agree their objectives and development aims with their managers, and adopt an active role with regards to them.'[14] Because of this shift, the role of human resources has changed from that of owner–administrator to one that aims to promote development, growth, and recognition: 'We work on developing skills in both colleagues and line managers. We migrated from an HR active role (almost owner) to try to build up accountability and ownership among managers and colleagues. The one thing that should not happen in this process is people filling forms but not acknowledging the importance and impact of performance management in their compensation, growth, career development, and recognition. Being accountable for our performance is the foundation for achieving our professional aspirations and becoming highly engaged with what we do.'[15]

In summary, Pfizer's human resources now regards performance management as a process not as a tool, and it functions as a facilitator and capability builder rather than an owner of an administrative role. By making these changes, human resources is able to connect performance management with the business strategy and with the firm's other talent management initiatives.

4.2 MAPPING DEVELOPMENT: BUILDING ON INDIVIDUALS' STRENGTHS

What is the best way to develop people, such that the firm has the highest possible impact on the individual's development and, in turn, the individual has the highest possible impact on the organization?

Put differently, which development processes and opportunities have the greatest impact when investing in an individual? These questions, which are explored by Nick Van Dam (2007, p. 19), might be the most critical questions to address in designing an organization's talent development process.

There are many answers to these questions. Most emphasize the importance of training and on-the-job experience (Rothwell & Kazanas, 2004; Cheese et al., 2008). However, while such practices may indeed be important, the next generation talent management requires a different approach. This book argues that the 80–20 Rule[16] of Pareto, the nineteenth-century Italian sociologist, provides valuable insights for talent development. Using Pareto's Rule, it is suggested that companies should focus 80% of their development efforts on honing individuals' few, but demonstrated, strengths, rather than on identifying and addressing their many weaknesses. Put differently, an organization should build on an individual's strengths rather than on his or her weaknesses. Because companies' development plans tend to focus on how to improve individuals' deficiencies rather than on how to build their strengths, applying Pareto's insights to talent development has the potential to revolutionize this area of talent management.

The strengths-based approach has been applied by a number of companies. The UK division of the aerospace company BAE Systems is one such example.[17] As a result of using this approach, managers at BAE Systems are now given those projects that they are naturally drawn to, that is, those projects that they enjoy and find energizing. Another company that has changed its focus from competencies to strengths is Norwich Union, the largest insurer in the UK.[18] The company initially implemented this change among claim advisers, who have a customer-service role. The company helped the group identify those strengths necessary to be a high-performing claims adviser. Once these strengths were spotted, the organization was able to recruit people who were made for the job rather than people who were able to do the job.[19]

Note that this book is not discarding the idea of learning, and addressing an individual's weaknesses. Rather, it is suggesting that a shift is needed to focus more attention on strengths when strategically mapping out individuals' development plans. To see the value of such a shift, consider, following Van Dam, the world of sports. In this world, athletes are encouraged to develop their strengths. Yet organizational performance systems tend to focus on developing competencies in those areas in which an individual is weak. As athletes know, building on strengths is the only way to gain an edge over one's competitors. Development should thus be focused mainly on identifying, assessing, and building on the core strengths of an organization's people.

In practice, this means that unlike the traditional competency approach, which requires that a person shows a certain level of competency for each skill, the strengths approach allows people to hone their strengths as much as possible while delivering at least a passing level of competency in other required skills.

The traditional competency approach uses many methods to evaluate competency. Among the most well known is GAP analysis. In traditional GAP analysis, different competencies are first ranked according to their relative importance for the position being analyzed. An individual's actual skill level is then assessed and compared against the target level of skill. The result is a GAP chart, such as that in Figure 4.6,[20] that takes into account both desired and actual skill levels.

The objective of this type of analysis is to make sure that, if an individual's actual skill level comes in below the target level, the difference or gap between these two levels shortens over time. Resources are therefore allocated to help managers and future leaders reach the standard desired. Feedback is also given accordingly.

The strength-based approach, in contrast, requires a different type of analysis. Specifically, highly valued strengths – strengths that work toward better performance on the job – are taken into account in

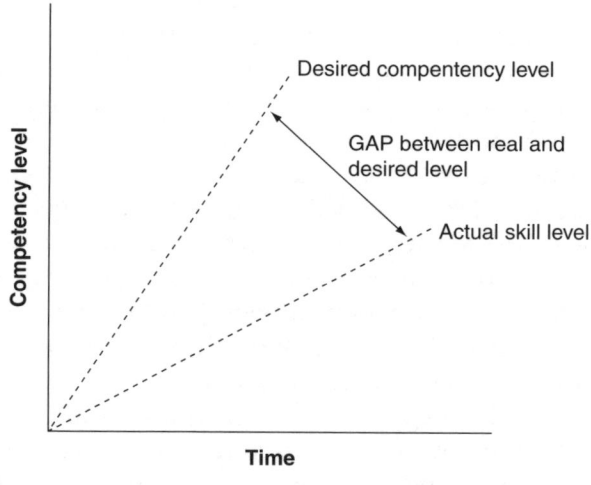

FIGURE 4.6 **GAP analysis**

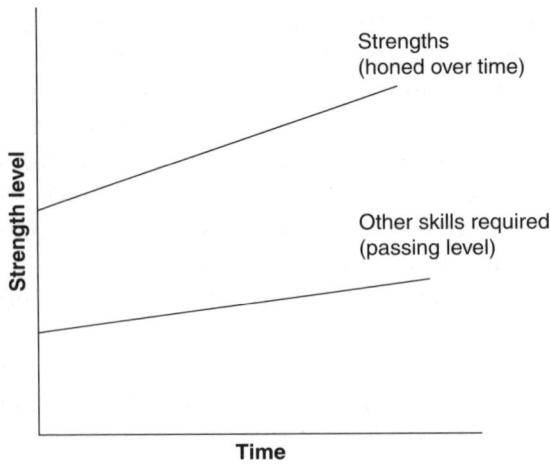

FIGURE 4.7 **The strength-based approach to development**

addition to minimum required levels of competency. This analysis then provides the basis for deciding which developmental and learning methods are best to apply to build on the individual's strengths. Figure 4.7 illustrates the strength-based approach to human capital development.

Implementing a strengths-based approach should help firms understand what the strength profiles are of various positions (as in the case of Norwich Union), how to recruit around these profiles to leverage individuals' talents, and how to remove the factors that might be constraining the optimal use of individuals' talents. This new method will change the way development is carried out, as it entails focusing on developing those skills and capabilities in which a person is able to outshine the rest. No more one-size-fits-all competencies and no more feedback in which individuals' weaknesses lead the development-planning discussion. Rather, strengths will dominate these discussions, with weaknesses to be tackled in a manner that enhances strengths. For many firms, this approach will be different and perhaps even unnatural, but it is the only one that can allow firms to respond to a rapidly changing context proactively and dynamically.

As suggested at the beginning of this section, the consequence of a good development process that facilitates learning is great performance. Learning allows people to expand their 'organizational capability by leveraging individuals' strengths, perspectives, and experiences'

(Cheese et al., 2008, p. 145). Learning can occur in different ways. For instance, one can acquire knowledge cognitively. One may also learn through experience, accumulating knowledge and skills by participating in different activities or projects. Finally, one can learn on an emotional level; the term 'emotional intelligence' refers to one's ability to manage one's own emotions or the emotions of others. Daniel Goleman (1995) has popularized this concept, stressing four emotional intelligence competencies: self-awareness; self-management; social-awareness; and relationship management.

Assuming that the organization has decided to focus its talent development efforts on building individuals' strengths, the next step is to identify which development activities will accomplish this goal. Table 4.1 maps various development activities to the different ways one can learn (cognition, experience, and emotional intelligence).[21]

Note that different types of development opportunities will be useful to professionals at different stages of their career. For instance, a young professional will benefit most from cognitive learning opportunities that teach the individual the tools necessary to perform his or her job well. As the professional reaches middle management, interpersonal skills and managerial abilities will begin to be important to the individual's success, and thus experience-based learning opportunities and opportunities to develop his or her emotional intelligence will become useful. At the managerial level, the individual's social abilities, network consolidation, and informal relationships will dominate the technical knowledge that was once so important. Energizers, for Cross et al. (2003) – those people who commit, connect, and try to find synergies between ideas and capabilities within the organization – have more chances to perform better than those who just bring knowledge and abilities. Senior managers will also benefit from continued opportunities to develop their emotional intelligence as well as from continued hands-on learning. Thus, the way an organization should deliver various learning opportunities over the course of a professional's career should depend on factors such as career stage and job responsibility.

At Royal Mail, development discussions with the firm's top team yielded a plan that focuses on five areas: skills; experience; exposure; feedback; and coaching. The Head of Leadership Development notes, 'We want people to be exposed to the right things, to the right people and to the right situations... if they are high-potential people, we want to make sure they are well-connected. At the same time, we want to

TABLE 4.1 **Developmental methods and how one learns**

Development activities	How one learns		
	Cognition (knowledge)	**Experience**	**Emotional intelligence**
Reading	X		
Foundational managerial education	X		
Leadership programs	X		
Professional conferences	X		
Classroom-based events	X		
e-learning	X		
Field trips	X		
Coaching support	X		
Think-tank experiences	X	X	
Line-to-staff switches	X	X	
Stretch assignments		X	
Turnaround projects		X	
Job assignment		X	
Role models			X
Feedback			X
Mentoring		X	X
Networks		X	X
360° feedback			X
Unfamiliar responsibilities		X	
Inherited problems		X	
Problems with employees			X
Increased scope and scale		X	
Influence without authority			X
Work across cultures		X	
Work group diversity		X	
Starting project from scratch		X	

make sure that they are reflecting on their performance, reflecting on their development, and continually learning.'[22]

Figure 4.8 summarizes how learning opportunities should be presented over the course of a professional's career.

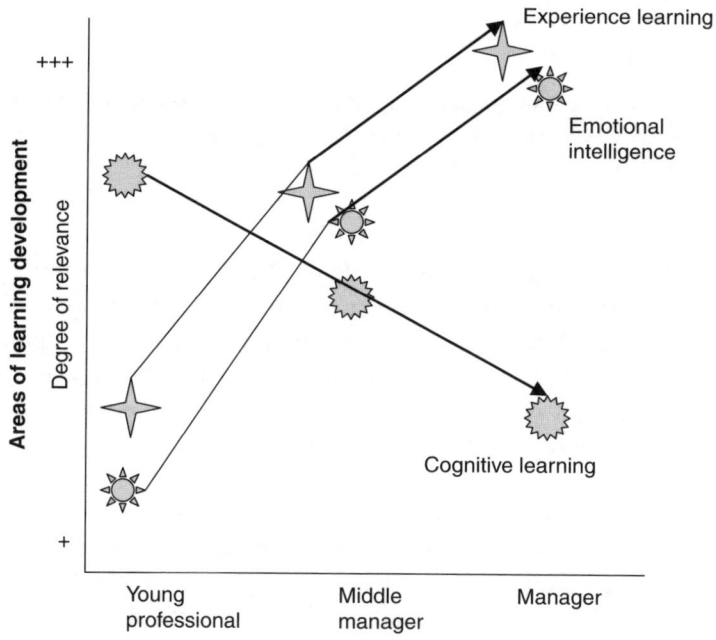

FIGURE 4.8 **Learning over time**

Off the record

Learning and technology: different approaches for different generations

Blogs, webinars, podcasts, online games, simulations, multimedia wikis: these are but a few of the media that Gen Yers use in their daily approach to learning and fun.

While Baby Boomers saw the first videos emerge, and Gen Xers witnessed the advent and growth of computers and the internet, Gen Yers were born plugged in to technology. Van Dam (2007) stresses the differences in different generations' attitudes towards learning and notes the impact these differences have in terms of collaborative problem-solving.

Gen Yers prefer to learn in networks or teams, where technology (such as multimedia) is an integral part of the learning experience. In addition, Gen Yers expect to be entertained during the process of learning. Thus, instead of boring classroom-style conferences, which Baby Boomers were accustomed to, the view among this generation is 'let's use simulations to have fun while learning first hand'.

(Continued)

As such, experiential learning opportunities are becoming critical at early stages of Gen Yers' careers as a way for organizations to release and track young professionals' potential.

Figure 4.9 is similar to Figure 4.8 in that it also summarizes how learning opportunities should be presented over the course of a professional's career. However, rather than plot career stage against the relevance of the three types of learning opportunity, Figure 4.9 plots career stage against competencies required and the learning activities that are necessary to develop these competencies.

As Figure 4.9 illustrates, technical competencies that are required at the beginning of one's career are supported by cognitive learning, whereas interpersonal competencies and managerial competencies that are required later in one's career are supported by both emotional intelligence and experience-based learning opportunities.

Figure 4.9 can be modified to present the different development activities listed in Table 4.1 that correspond to the three types of

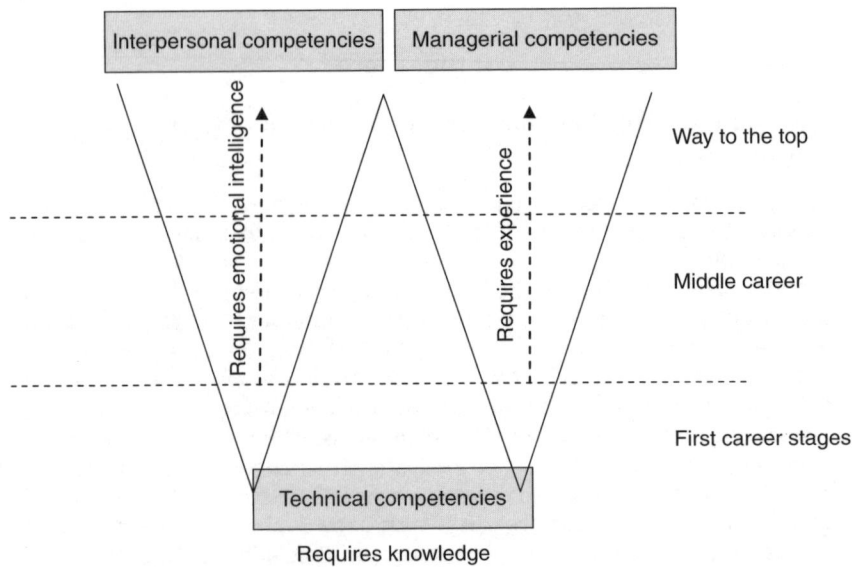

FIGURE 4.9 **Competencies and learning opportunities by career stage**

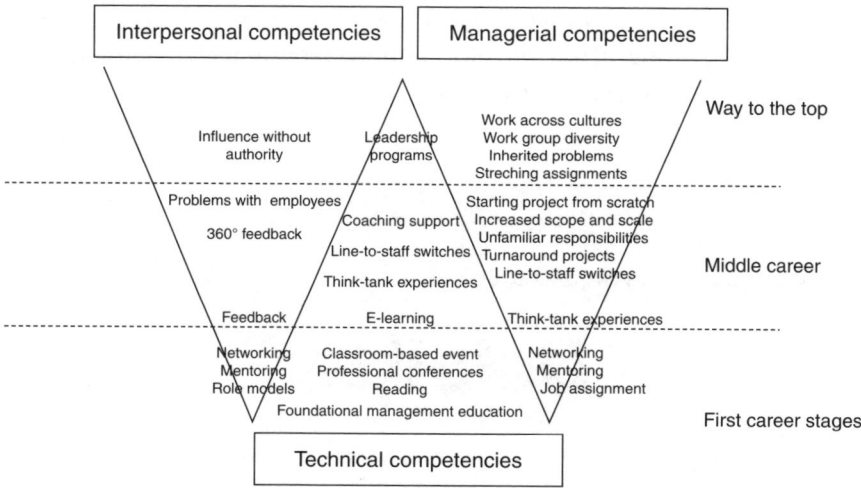

FIGURE 4.10 **Competencies and development activities by career stage**

learning opportunities. Figure 4.10 therefore depicts which development activities are required at different stages of a professional's career within an organization.

So how should organizations design development plans around the above development activities? One option is to use a structured development program. Structured programs have the advantage that they can send employees a common message; however, while they are often successful at levelling knowledge discrepancies through the provision of cognitive learning opportunities, they tend to have trouble tackling more complex issues related to experience-based or emotional intelligence-related learning opportunities. Another option is to use the nine-grid box to clarify which development activities are most appropriate for the different groups within the matrix. Alternatively, companies may decide to prepare a specific development program for 'stars'. Whatever development program is chosen, organizations must remember to customize some of the activities so as to enhance individuals' strengths. For example, a firm may decide that those people located in the 'start' box of the matrix should go through a strategic leadership program as well as be placed in a stretch assignment. Some people within this group may then demonstrate an ability to deal with people at different levels of the organization. The company should next present these individuals an opportunity to lead another diverse group. In proceeding in this fashion, companies will be able to build on general competencies among the 'star' group, while providing a well thought-out developmental experience that focuses on individuals' demonstrated strengths.

Best practices at a glance

Deloitte: a learning organization

Deloitte.

With more than 169,000 employees and aggregate Member Firm revenues of US$26.1 bn,[23] Deloitte is the brand under which tens of thousands of dedicated professionals in independent firms throughout the world collaborate to provide audit, consulting, financial advisory, risk management, and tax services to selected clients. These firms are members of Deloitte Touche Tohmatsu (DTT), a Swiss Verein. Each member firm provides services in a particular geographic area and is subject to the laws and professional regulations of the particular country or countries in which it operates. The firm is considered a leader in the professional services industry.

The arrival of a new generation in the workforce (approximately 60% of the firm's workforce are Millennials, also known as Generation Y, born after 1981) has made the firm realize that 'when people consider an employer, one thing they look for is a place where they can take their set of skills to the next level, a place where they can develop, explore their talents, and grow their career. Deloitte is a learning organization, which is a place where people are encouraged to learn new things, stretch themselves, and have the opportunity to develop.'[24] This happens through a combination of formal learning, informal learning, and on-the-job learning and development.

To support this, Deloitte has implemented a global learning platform which provides all its people around the world with unlimited, 24/7 access to over 60,000 technology-based learning solutions, including online books, web-based training programs, simulations and games, webinars, online coaching and mentoring, video-based learning, social networks, podcasts, and learning wikis, among other resources. As a result, people are connected to a wealth of knowledge, latest thinking, and to each other. Another example of a strategic talent development capability is the 'Deloitte Virtual Classroom'. This industry-leading, live learning platform offers the ability to conduct live, instructor-led classes online. Through the Deloitte Virtual Classroom, people around the world can participate in live training without the need for travel.

Learning and development through the global learning platforms is a strategic component of Deloitte's talent development strategy because it 'supports to attract people, is part of the value proposition for talent, and has an impact on retention and knowledge creation'.[25]

In this book, discussions on talent management so far have tried to knock down a few old paradigms that might not help organizations to be as flexible or innovative as they need to be given rapid changes in the market. For instance, it has highlighted the importance of both rising from within, as a means of developing experienced talent, and hiring, as a means of bringing fresh ideas into the firm. The book has also emphasized the importance of broadening the scope of development by combining succession planning with talent pool strategies. Doing so can help organizations spot and make use of the best talent when it is needed, rather than limit talent changes according to the readiness of those in the succession pipeline.

Besides knocking down old paradigms this book has also tried to connect different processes. For example, it has suggested that performance and potential analyses should be looked at together when identifying talent. It has also recommended that development focuses on leveraging individuals' strengths rather than their weaknesses, which requires that development be connected to different types of learning opportunities (i.e., cognitive, experience-based, and emotional intelligence). The connection between generically structured and individually tailored activities is also required to develop talent to the maximum.

Table 4.2 summarizes the old and new development realities discussed in this chapter.

The 'case in point' for this chapter analyzes development and learning at Syngenta, and shows how the various facets of talent management can be integrated into a company's talent strategy. In turn, it illustrates how the firm's talent management strategy works to further the organization's success.

Chapter 5 will focus on talent retention. The analysis undertaken in Chapter 5 will build on earlier discussions of talent attraction and development, and show that a good foundation in terms of development is the key to retention success.

TABLE 4.2 **The old and new development realities**

Old talent development paradigms	Developing people in the next generation of talents
Raise from within	Raise from within and hire from the market
Focus on succession planning (filling a leadership pipeline)	Focus on succession planning and talent pools
Evaluate performance and potential separately	Performance and potential analysis connected
Focus on areas of improvement	Focus on enhancing strengths
Development is a series of activities	Development connects with learning
Use structured development programs	Use flexible development programs

CASE IN POINT: SYNGENTA

Syngenta: talent development

In 2000, Novartis and Astrazeneca merged their agribusinesses to form Syngenta (from the Greek 'Syn' synergy and 'Genta' humanity and individuals), the first global group dedicated exclusively to agribusiness.[26] With more than 25,000 employees in 90 countries, in 2009 Syngenta's sales were US$10,992 million.

The company's main businesses are crop protection, seeds, and lawn and garden. Figure 4.11[27] details some of the segments within these three businesses.

At Syngenta, development and learning are an integral part of the company's talent management strategy. Talent management is no longer limited to just 'top talent', but rather there are multiple layers of talent (see Figure 4.12) in which high potentials, whether generalists or specialists, are found. Potential for the firm is a combination of aspiration, engagement, and ability. Those individuals who are considered high potentials are the main focus of the firm's development efforts.

Syngenta links its development activities to the following three types of learning: experience-based learning; relationship-based learning;

Syngenta has three businesses

Crop protection	Seeds	Lawn & garden*

Selective herbicides	Corn & soybean	Flowers
Non-selective herbicides	Diverse field crops	Growing media
Fungicides	Vegetables	Chemical controls
Insecticides		Turf & ornamentals
Seed care		
Professional products		

FIGURE 4.11 **Syngenta's three businesses**

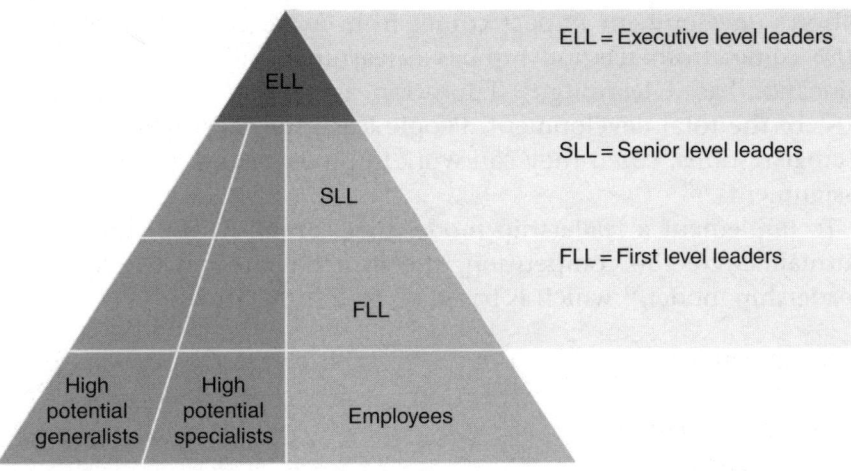

ELL = Executive level leaders

SLL = Senior level leaders

FLL = First level leaders

ELL

SLL

FLL

High potential generalists | High potential specialists | Employees

FIGURE 4.12 **Layers of talent**

and education-based learning. Experience-based learning opportunities are largely provided by job changes and development in role. Relationship-based learning opportunities are delivered via the use of role models, coaching, and ongoing feedback. Finally, education-based learning is supported by formal training programs. Figure 4.13 details some of the development activities associated with these three types of learning at Syngenta.[28]

Experience-based learning

Job changes: reorganizations, changes in scope/scale of responsibilities, job rotations.

Development in role: project/taskforce assignments, professional communities, knowledge networks.

Relationship-based learning

Ongoing feedback: performance reviews, self-assessment, 360° feedback, development centers.

Role models and coaching: role modelling, coaching, mentoring.

Education-based learning

Formal training: PC/Web-based learning modules, educational programs/seminars, conferences.

FIGURE 4.13 **Development activities associated with the three types of learning**

In terms of the weight the company gives these different types of development activities, in the company's view, 70% of the organization's development impact comes from experience-based learning, 20% comes from relationship-based learning, and 10% comes from education-based learning.[29] 'Education as such . . . only contributes 10% of the total development. People learn the most when they can change options, when they can work in projects, and get challenging assignments.'[30]

To implement a leadership model that can allow the company to outmanoeuvre the competition, the firm has created the Syngenta Leadership model,[31] which is based on four imperatives:

- Set directions
- Drive results
- Liberate potential
- Create edge.

Each of these imperatives is linked to a set of leadership competencies that managers should be developing. For instance, 'set directions' is associated with competencies that include defining the business strategy, encouraging innovation, acquiring business know-how, and communicating effectively.

Note that Syngenta is careful to make sure that the above imperatives, competencies, development activities, and types of learning are well connected to each other. For instance, the company provides

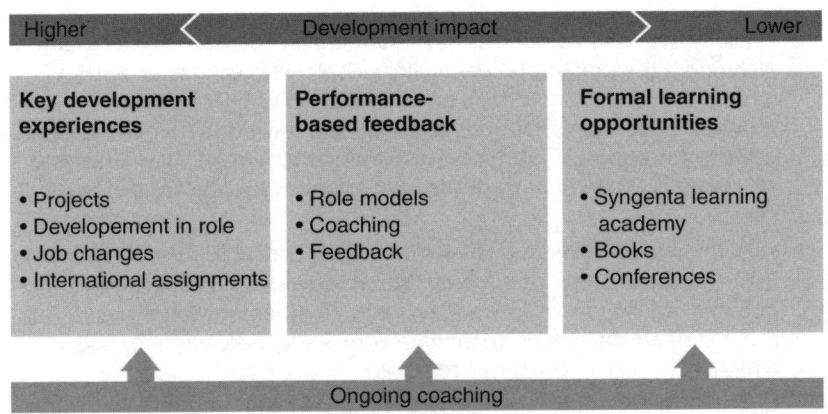

FIGURE 4.14 **Development and learning at Syngenta**

its managers with a development guide that gives examples of different types of assignments.[32] In so doing, each manager can see which learning areas and development activities are necessary to develop the competencies required of the four imperatives. Figure 4.14 illustrates that all development and learning activities should be supported by ongoing coaching in order to maximize their effectiveness.

As Syngenta's Leader Development Guide observes, 'You need to integrate things. You cannot talk about development alone forgetting about the rest of the activities that are critical for talent management. The challenge for us and for companies [in general] is to tightly integrate the old practices into the new wheel of talent management. Development is critical for a good talent management strategy and our aim is also to facilitate managers' experience in terms of development and make sure leaders and employees are responsible for development.'[33]

CHAPTER HIGHLIGHTS

❖ Raising from within and hiring from the market is no longer an either-or choice. Rather, they are complements, with the latter necessary to moderate the effects of market swings or of people leaving to pursue new challenges elsewhere.

❖ Similarly, whereas companies have traditionally focused on succession planning – the practice of identifying people who can fill leadership roles in the future – in today's next generation of talent era companies should also develop talent pools: groups of individuals that companies develop for a specific job. These activities complement each other and are necessary to benefit from the right talent as such talent becomes critical.

❖ Performance and potential analysis are both critical to identify talent. Performance analysis looks backwards at individuals' past actions; potential analysis looks forward and asks whether individuals are capable of advancement, managing complexity and learning, and whether they share the firm's core values.

❖ Cognitive learning, experience-based learning, and emotional learning support the development process over individuals' careers by strengthening their interpersonal, managerial, and technical competencies, respectively.

VERY IMPORTANT QUESTIONS

❧ Is your organization making talent, buying talent, or both?

❧ With respect to filling the leadership pipeline, is the focus on succession planning, talent pools, or both?

❧ Has your company established a reliable performance assessment process?

❧ Are performance and potential appraisals used to analyze and identify talent?

❧ Do your company's development programs aim to boost individuals' strengths? Or is the focus on addressing weaknesses?

❧ Do your organization's development activities support professionals at different career stages?

5

TALENT MANAGEMENT STEP 3: A LONG-TERM RETENTION MODEL

This chapter discusses employee retention. Retention, defined by Frank et al. (2004, p. 13) as 'the effort by an employer to keep desirable workers in order to meet business objectives', is an inclusive concept that includes both tangible and intangible factors. Many of these factors can negatively affect retention, for instance, weak engagement, low levels of motivation, a high degree of distrust, a lack of communication or transparency, or poorly managed compensation and reward practices, to mention a few. Obviously, the more time and money a company puts into developing talent, the more important it becomes to retain the talent so as to observe a return on this investment. Retention is also important, however, to avoid the hidden costs of turnover, such as loss of knowledge and experience.

Retaining talent requires long-term thinking and creative planning. Most employee retention programs focus on developing attractive benefits packages, which often include features such as holiday pay, schedule adjustments, and competitive compensation. However, benefits packages are not sufficient to address turnover problems and thus, such focus prevents organizations from developing a holistic view of turnover issues and, in turn, truly effective retention practices.

A recent study[1] reveals that 10% of the global workforce is disenchanted with their organizations. These individuals have low intellectual, emotional or motivational connections with the firm. As such, they are likely to leave the company as soon as an opportunity arises. Meanwhile, dissatisfied employees are not likely to perform well; for instance, they may put off customers (internal and external) or provide low-quality service. Hence, in addition to offering competitive benefits packages, it is imperative that organizations tackle more complex turnover issues when trying to retain employees. Put differently,

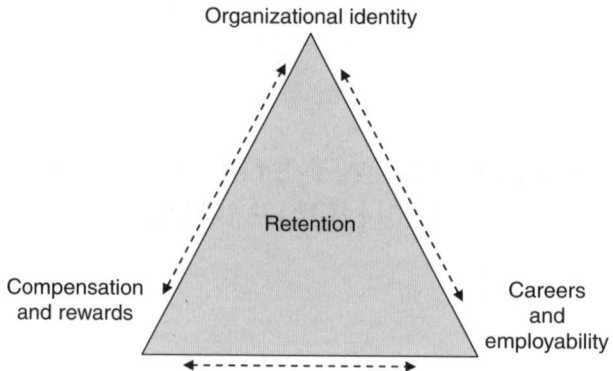

FIGURE 5.1 **A model for a long-term retention strategy**

an organization's retention program should focus on other issues besides those related to short-term extrinsic motivations that influence individuals' decisions to stay…or to leave. This therefore requires a strategic, long-term focus.

The model for long-term retention featured in this book includes three elements: the typical compensation and rewards used (and abused) by firms, as well as two additional sets of factors that are considered equally important in today's market; organizational identity on the one hand, and careers and employability on the other. Together, these three sets of factors can closely connect the employee to the firm by respectively improving the recognition, commitment, and engagement sought by both parties. Figure 5.1 summarizes this model.

The next three sections discuss these three sets of factors in turn.

5.1 ORGANIZATIONAL IDENTITY = COMMITMENT

Why does the concept of organizational identity emerge as an important factor in understanding retention? And what are the main features of this concept? Lastly, how does this all tie together?

Albert & Whetten (1985) characterize organizational identity as having three dimensions: first, what is considered central to the organization; second, what makes the organization distinctive; and third, what is enduring about the organization from the perspective of its members, that is, what links the organization's present with its past.

At the heart of this definition are the core values that make organizations act or react in a particular way and the lenses through
which managers interpret organizational issues (Dutton & Penner,
1993; Collins & Porras, 2000; Gioia & Thomas, 1996).

Consistent with this characterization, this book focuses on an organization's values rather than its culture in discussing organizational
identity. One reason for this choice is that the former can be more
sharply differentiated than the latter, facilitating organizational analysis (Alvesson, 1987). Another reason is that, while culture focuses
on an organization's symbols and beliefs (Pettigrew, 1979), values are
more central to the organization as well as more enduring (Albert &
Whetten, 1985), and thus are more likely to lead to commitment
among the members of an organization.

In their examination of 18 long-lasting firms that they term 'visionary firms', Collins & Porras (2000) conclude that visionary companies
are those that can articulate a core ideology. By defining a set of
core values, companies develop a clear, stable identity that allows
people to identify with the company and in turn increases commitment (Hatum et al., 2008). In turn, by consolidating employees'
commitment behind the company's core values, companies' organizational identity is strengthened (Hatum & Pettigrew, 2006; Hatum,
2007). Thus, while a visionary company's business strategy may change
in accordance with market conditions, its identity remains intact.
This echoes Gagliardi's (1986) proposition that the primary strategy of an organization should be the maintenance of its cultural
identity.

Briefly, by ensuring that their values remain largely unchanged
throughout different generations, firms can forge a very strong identity and thus a sense of coherence among their people. Such coherence
gives the people a sense of identity and commitment towards the organization's set of values, mission, and beliefs. The role of the founders
in creating such a set of beliefs (i.e., values) and in consolidating the
people's commitment behind those values allows the companies to
achieve a strong organizational identity (Hatum & Pettigrew, 2006;
Hatum, 2007).

The importance of a stable identity is highlighted by Gustafson &
Reger (1995). In their study, the authors argue that an organization's
identity consists of two sets of attributes: intangible attributes, which
are central and enduring (e.g., core values), and substantive attributes,
which include the organization's products, strategies, and geographical

scope. Gustafson & Reger (1995) show that in times of turmoil, when organizations seek to adapt to new environmental circumstances, the substantive attributes change while the intangible elements remain unchanged. Thus, for Gustafson & Reger, the result is that organizations are able to adapt to changing conditions while simultaneously maintaining stability by using their identity as a psychological anchor.

The role of organizational identity during times of turmoil is critical for a firm's survival. Consider, for example, the case of AGD (Aceitera General Deheza), an Argentine edible oil firm, one of the main oil exporters in the country. The company underwent a huge organizational transformation starting in 1990, when the firm diversified its business portfolio and adopted a business unit structure. By creating a set of beliefs (or values) and consolidating employees' commitment to those values, the company's founders ensured that the firm's values remained largely unchanged throughout different generations of the organization's structure. This worked to help AGD forge a very strong identity. Yet the strong identity of AGD did not trap the company into a set of rigid inertial forces. On the contrary, because AGD's identity was grounded in values such as agile decision-making and innovation – values related to the positive aspects of change – the firm was able to transform itself quickly and smoothly. That is, AGD's values enabled the company to undertake major transformation without damaging its core identity and hence without resistance to change. Thus, by maintaining the firm's core values, it was able to change its strategies, products, and processes without creating internal turmoil. Interviews with a representative of the company were revealing in this respect: 'Over the 1990s the company changed a lot. However, if you ask an employee whether they have felt the changes, they would say that they had not noticed internal turmoil. They did not feel threatened by the changes. I do not know how or why this has happened. However, if you compared our business now and ten years ago, you would think we were a different company.'[2]

So how does a strong organizational identity lead to increased commitment and, in turn, long-term retention? One possibility is that the stronger an organization's values, the more likely managers' words and actions will align. Such alignment not only gives a sense of coherence, but also inspires employees. Employees, as Aselstine & Alletson (2006, p. 6) point out, want to see the organization's vision and mission put into practice by managers and 'visible leaders'. A strong identity can also engender trust and loyalty, making people feel more at ease when a crisis arises. Finally, a clear and strong identity provides one with a sense of stability and continuity, which people tend to value. Thus, such an identity will strengthen firms' retention prospects.

According to a Tower Perrin study,[3] top retention drivers across generations in the workplace are: the satisfaction they receive with organizational decisions concerning people; the good relationship with supervisors; and the organization's reputation as a great place to work. Commitment requires not only writing down organizational values, but also demonstrating them on a daily basis.

After working to create a strong identity, the next step in designing a successful retention plan is to link this process to a transparent and fair system of compensation and rewards that recognizes people according to their contributions to the organization. Such systems are discussed in the next section.

The case of Bimbo facilitates the understanding of how a company can balance organizational identity and retention goals.

Best practices at a glance

Bimbo: strong identity and coherence

'To be a highly productive and completely humane company'[4] – this is the philosophy of Grupo Bimbo, a global firm with headquarters in Mexico that has more than 100 plants worldwide, 104,000 employees, and US$ 7.4 bn of net sales. Founded in 1945, Bimbo is one of the most important baking companies in terms of trademark positioning, sales, and production volume around the world.[5]

At Bimbo, the words Believe and Create are viewed as both fundamental and interrelated: to create quality products, a belief in the company's values is important; in turn, creating quality products is important to believe in the company's values. These values (passion, profitability, teamwork, effectiveness, quality, and trust) locate the individual as the central actor.

The importance the company gives to the individual, and the potential benefit of doing so, is illustrated by the comments of Roberto Servitje, one of

(Continued)

the company's founders, in reflecting upon a management program at Harvard University: 'In one of the last subjects, we went through a simulation. We worked in teams and we had to manage and make decisions about different situations. One of those decisions, which was a turning point for our fictitious firm... was when sales dropped. Very quickly, an American colleague suggested firing some blokes. I rejected that idea, and along with a Japanese colleague we argued "they are not blokes, they are people and we are not going to fire them". Later, the market went up and we won the simulation. The rest of the groups had fired people but when the market recovered they had to hire and train people again. This would take time; however, we were ready and took advantage [of the market upturn].'[6]

To link the company's values with the work environment, Bimbo offers various training programs. One of the training courses must be taken within the first two years of working at the company. During three days employees reflect on different issues such as the person, their ideal, spirituality, health, mankind, the organization, work, and society. 'Throughout the course people deepen their "ideal", asking themselves questions such as what am I doing in this world? What is my essence? Some people realize they are not fit for this company.'[7]

Bimbo tries to clearly and transparently convey its organizational values that allow employees to identify and connect with the company, leading in turn to sustained growth in a changing environment.

Off the record

Talent fed up with corporate life

The British comedy series *The Office* features an office environment that nobody would envy[8] – the boss is a bully with questionable leadership skills, jobs are demotivating, and employees are careless. Unfortunately, the skewing social satire is not far from the reality that many employees are exposed to in corporate offices around the world today, and many talented people are fed up with these boring and stressful environments, full of political plays and less-than-rewarding jobs.

In *Escape from Corporate America*, Pamela Skillings (2008) aims to help Americans get out of the corporate nightmare. Coining the term 'corporate disillusionment', which she defines as a 'sinking feeling that there is no way out', escaping is the best alternative according to the author. However, alternatives to the choice between tolerating a toxic work environment or escaping are starting to emerge. For instance, a recent article[9] on new ways of working points to the development of 'jellies', which are shared working spaces outside the corporate office in which 15 to 20 people gather to work. By fostering a more creative and stimulating work environment these shared workspaces have led to greater motivation and, as a result, companies such as Yahoo! are starting to sponsor some of them. Such innovations in work environments might be especially good news for the younger generation of workers.

5.2 COMPENSATION AND REWARDS = RECOGNITION

Talented people want to be paid according to market standards. In addition, they want to be rewarded for their performance either monetarily or through some other kind of recognition. Accordingly, a firm's compensation and rewards are commonly used as part of a company's strategy to retain people. However, so many mistakes have been made in implementing such programs that firms have undermined their potential.

For instance, companies sometimes increase an employee's compensation in order to avoid losing talent that threatens to leave. But doing so can lead to a feeling of unfairness among the other employees. In other cases, firms try to distinguish their employees by segmenting them, offering different compensation and rewards to different 'players' or forcing rankings so that 'premium' employees can be rewarded accordingly (Lawler III, 2008; Sears, 2003).

Every company has some form of compensation and reward strategy. It may be formally or informally stated. The main difference across such strategies comes down to whether the firm integrates a comprehensive compensation system with a more holistic retention strategy, and in turn with its talent management strategy. In order to achieve such a goal, companies have to go beyond their current compensation practices.

In the next generation talent management era, compensation and rewards should be tied to the company's analysis of performance and potential. The matrix introduced in Figure 4.5 can be a good tool for outlining a company's compensation and reward policies, as it provides an easy way to segment people.

Two issues are paramount when designing compensation and rewards that support a long-term retention strategy: the flexibility of the system, and the incentives of the system. A flexible system can adapt compensation and rewards to different types of talent (as identified, for example, by a performance and potential matrix). In contrast, rigidities in pay structure can be a significant hurdle to introducing new forms of organizing that might allow firms to succeed in a context of rapid change (Child, 2005). A retention-enhancing system will deliver compensation and rewards in a manner that increases individual and group performance-related incentives to stay with the firm and deliver good performance.

Figure 5.2 shows how an organization can design a flexible, incentives-based compensation and rewards system by using a performance and potential matrix.

In Figure 5.2, those talents deemed to be vital to the future of the company, and hence who may also be of value to competing firms, are located in the top right of the matrix. To increase the likelihood of retaining these people, the organization should establish a

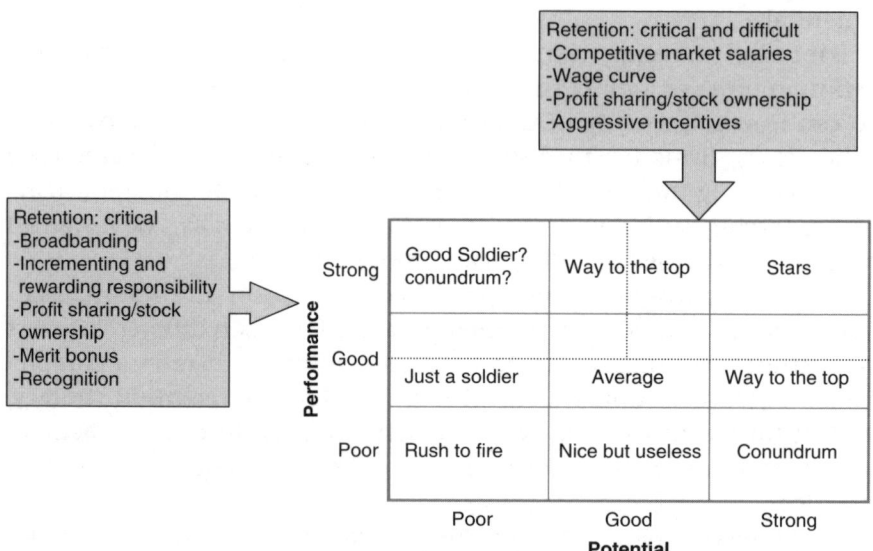

FIGURE 5.2 **Performance and potential matrix and the design of a flexible, incentives-based compensation and rewards system**

wage curve that ensures competitive salaries (in relation to the industry and the general market) and it should aggressively use incentives such as stock options. In doing so the organization provides both long- and short-term motivations for star talent to stay with the company.

Other players in the matrix are also important. For example, those in the top left are also critical for the business, as they typically have a wealth of technical or professional expertise. Some of these individuals might be future star performers. However, others may lack the motivation or aptitude to take over larger or more complex jobs in the future, and hence they may remain in their position for a long time. It is therefore necessary for the organization to be creative in terms of how to use compensation and rewards to also retain these individuals. By flexibly using broadbanding, incremental responsibility, merit bonuses, and stock ownership, an organization may be better able to retain this segment.

Different companies may include or exclude different components of a compensation system depending on the possibilities available to them, their culture, and their ownership structure (i.e., family firms, public companies, etc).

Notice that above it states that to support a retention strategy, compensation and rewards should be delivered in a manner that increases both individual and group performance-related incentives. Which is to say that in addition to individual incentives, group-based incentives such as business unit-based bonuses, team bonuses or profit sharing should be part of an organization's retention plan (Lawler III, 2008). Organizations looking for ways to retain their best talent have to make sure that this talent is involved in the organizational life so as not to foster an environment of mercenaries spreading the seeds of discontent. A combination of individual and group-based performance rewards can help firms root their talent into the organizational life. Earlier the relevance of a common set of values to shaping an organization's identity was highlighted and, in turn, to increasing retention. Bringing people together through the compensation system can contribute to connecting people to a shared set of values.

In general terms, it is suggested that a company follows a pay-for-performance model, such as that depicted in Figure 5.3.

The first step of the model in Figure 5.3 corresponds to the individual: individual employees should receive lump sum bonuses according

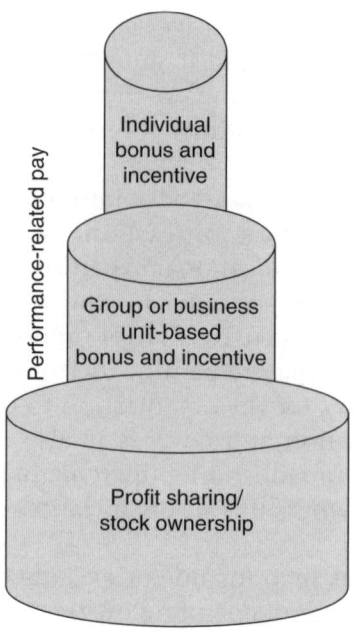

FIGURE 5.3 **A pay-for-performance model**

to their own performance so as to motivate them to deliver optimal performance. The second step corresponds to group or business-unit bonuses: attachment to a business unit or group allows the employee to also be rewarded as the group's overall performance improves or otherwise meets some target. Whether such rewards take the form of a group bonus or a business unit-based bonus will depend on the company's size and structure. 'Gain sharing', which ties pay to increased productivity or cost savings, can be applied at this level. Usually this method is limited to an assembly line, a factory plant or a group of people working in a project. The third step corresponds to 'profit sharing' or stock ownership. The former rewards employees when the firm observes increased profits, whereas the latter is a form of long-term pay that also increases as the firm's overall performance in the market improves.

To summarize, each of the above levels of performance pay should be interconnected and aligned with the business strategy. Although it may seem that group-based rewards are only weakly related to an individual's results, they help ensure that the organization is not just a collection of talented people but rather an organization of highly involved people, which corresponds more tightly to retention. Further, a combination of short- and long-term pay methods is required. Short-term compensation and rewards help incentivize performance, whereas long-term compensation and rewards root people to the organization. The 'case in point' analyzed at the end of this chapter illustrates how a compensation and rewards strategy can be designed to work in concert with a firm's overall talent management strategy.

Thus far, this book has discussed how organizational identity works to increase commitment and how flexible compensation and rewards can work to increase incentivizing recognition. These factors are important to retaining talent. However, they are not the whole story.

Companies tend to display an extrinsic incentive bias, which means that they overestimate the extent to which employees care about extrinsic motivation such as pay, and underestimate the role of intrinsic motivation that stems from factors such as the appeal of the corporate culture, the motivation associated with the purpose of the firm, opportunities for learning and growth, and promotion opportunities. An individual's employability or career path with the firm is also central to an employee's decision of whether to stay with the company. In today's labor market, career paths have moved away from traditional paradigms, affecting the engagement and continuity of good employees that once ruled the job market. New career models that are relevant for creating engagement and, in turn, higher retention, are the subject of the next section.

5.3 EMPLOYABILITY/CAREER PATHS = ENGAGEMENT

In earlier discussions on development and learning, emphasis was given to the relevance of the stage in which the person's career is at. Careers or career paths themselves are important, however, because they have changed in complexity over time. This is especially important when one considers both the relationship between careers and different generations, and the complexity of the changes that organizations have gone through over time. It would be difficult for companies to generate a solid next generation of leaders without comprehension of how individuals' career paths have changed.

Since companies have become flatter, more linear, more flexible or whatever other euphemism for 'organizational cutback' you prefer to use, individuals' careers have had to adapt to a less orthodox career path than was once the norm. Moreover, many of the generational changes mentioned earlier have made the old career paradigms obsolete.

People are no longer focused simply on obtaining employment. Rather, the focus has shifted to employability, where employability is defined by Brown & Hesketh (2004, p. 25) as one's 'relative chances of getting and maintaining different kinds of employment'. Thus, rather than simply trying to find a job, people are now trying to find the conditions that will help them become more marketable. This is because people have realized that conditions in the labor market have changed. In particular, they will not get a job and stay with the hiring firm for the duration of their career, for this is not the 1950s, when organizations had a ladder to climb and people had the patience to wait. Rather, this is the new millennium, characterized by a scarcity of talent and widespread economic crises, and today's organizations are trying to cope with the market turmoil (and avoid going bust) by 'reorganizing'. As a result, many people have lost faith in their organizations and they no longer view frequent job changes negatively (sometimes they have no alternative!). Therefore, as the idea of a job for life is fading, employees are recognizing the need to maintain their employability. If a position will not enable them to develop skills that will ensure that they will remain marketable, they will seek other learning opportunities elsewhere (Aselstine & Alletson, 2006; Capelli, 1999). Opportunities to acquire knowledge and experience are thus imperative to entice people to join and stay with a firm.

The foregoing description of the current labor market might seem bleak, with employees lacking commitment, job-hopping, and seeking development and learning opportunities to further their employability, and with that companies are suffering from scarcity of talent and a certain amount of disdain from candidates that find companies a necessary evil. In this context, engaging people requires a different approach towards developing employees' careers.

The engagement challenge for organizations is to think about how employees feel about their work experience (Frank et al., 2004). Forget about lifetime employment; this is not only an old-fashioned idea but promoting it would mean that your organization has not yet understood the shift in professionals' minds. People look for a place where they can continuously learn and develop so they can always meet current market requirements.

At AON, a leading provider of risk-management services, insurance, and reinsurance, the objectives of the graduate program aim to engage new generations of employees through opportunities to work in different areas of the firm that have different subcultures and managers. First, the program encourages cross-selling, so that graduates learn to feel comfortable sitting with a client and having a conversation about their business. Second, the program helps its participants feel as if they are part of a networked population of future leaders. Third, the program gives these employees experiential learning opportunities that are 'highly energising, very engaging... have a very strong commercial edge and give them stimulus across the organization, with a mentor sponsor. The program offers access to key people, networks and experiences. We offer a project not only a job. [Younger generations] have a much greater purpose than just their immediate job. So in a way, we are trying to deliver in the program all those motivational drivers that Gen Yers tend to look for.'[10]

In his book *Beyond Certainty* (1996), Charles Handy took a stab at forecasting the future of careers. He coined the term 'portfolio class', which includes self-managers with their own assets, and argued that to attract and retain such talent firms had to abandon the upward organizational design, offering employees 'a continuing series of good roles if they want to keep their best people' (1996, p. 28).

Building on Handy's concept of a portfolio class, a career portfolio might be a useful concept to companies thinking about how to engage people within their organizations. The idea of a career portfolio resembles that of a financial portfolio. Just as a financial portfolio is a collection of investments with different risks that are employed to generate an investment return, people have diverse experiences and skills that they can apply in their job. In either case, the combination of assets or skills in the portfolio affects the investment or employability outcome. As discussed, people are keen to enhance their abilities to maintain long-term employability. Companies can implement this concept by offering a wide range of development experiences that capitalize on individuals' skills. In such a context, talent is more likely to want to stay with the organization longer. Of course, this requires that companies identify professionals' current versus desired skills, so that the opportunities that are offered engage as well as connect them to the organization.

An example of a company that manages a career portfolio is L'Oréal. The company is well aware of how career paths have transformed over time given its large focus on hiring young professionals. However, notwithstanding this transformation, the company continues to pursue the same objective that made it a great company: encouraging long-term commitment and engagement between the firm and the individual. L'Oréal's large brand portfolio can offer different business challenges to different people at different stages of their careers: 'Because you work on different brands or in different markets or different countries you will find challenges there, and that keeps the stimulus and the sense of finding something new within our different companies. We know that today a young person will say "I will be here for some time and then I will need something else". But, you can find "something else" inside our company... Our message to young people is "you can make a bet with us and we can keep you stimulated for 5, 10 or 15 years".'[11]

To some extent, employees are also increasingly looking for flexibility in their career possibilities. Some flexible arrangements that seek to retain people include flexi-time, part-time jobs, telecommuting, and leaves of absence, among others. But flexible arrangements can backfire on those joining the program by ruining their chances of promotion or even questioning the commitment of those involved in the program (Benko & Weisberg, 2007).

A new concept that has emerged that might boost retention is that of 'mass career customization' (Benko & Weisberg, 2007), also known as 'total career customization' (Tulgan, 2002). This concept aims to increase flexibility but at the same time takes into account a long-term career perspective. By mass career customization, Benko & Weisberg (2007) refer to the idea of a multiple career path that can be broken down into four dimensions: pace; workload; location; and role. According to this concept, a person may accelerate or decelerate the pace of his or her career progression, choose to have a full or reduced workload, restrict or expand the amount of work-related travel, and take on more or less responsibility. This approach replaces the 'career ladder' with a 'career lattice', thereby increasing alternative ways for high-potential employees along with great performers to stay in the organization but at a pace or along a path that suits them at any given point in time. Put differently, these career lattices can allow companies to enjoy the fruits of those employees who want to stay at the organization, while also respecting their employees' life and professional cycles.

Mass career customization has been tested and supported at Deloitte within the consulting business unit. As Benko & Weisberg (2007, p. 127) discuss, the decision to introduce this system to the consulting business unit was motivated by the fact that it tends to be the most travel intensive of the company's businesses, with the most geographically dispersed office locations and the least predictable workload among all the businesses. The results of this implementation were excellent: mass career customization and retention were positively correlated, morale and productivity rose, and a more positive and sustainable work–life balance was achieved.

Similarly, BAT (British American Tobacco) has looked at ways to depart from the old-fashioned ideas of career planning. 'With the concept of a career path, we give people an idea of how you can move up through the organization, but we realized that, these days, this is no longer valid...Organizations are becoming flatter and flatter, so there would be less positions to move up to, but people can continue to grow...It used to be very role-focused; to everybody's question "what is my next role", the answer was "usually one grade higher". What is more important [now] is "how am I going to improve my capabilities...what kind of challenges do I need to improve a specific capability?" [So] we look at what opportunities are out there in the different roles at different places that can offer those challenges.'[12]

BAT's new career development plan consists of five key dimensions: interpersonal skills; strategic; business; commercial; and functional. For example, if a person seeks to become a manager and he or she has never managed a large team, that person will need people-management experience, and hence the goal will be to find a role that can offer such experience. Similarly, if the person has not had commercial business experience and his or her career development plan requires such capability, the new role needs to offer a capability bridge between the individual's current and desired capabilities.

BAT's driving force to apply this flexible scheme was motivated in part by changing expectations about career pace: '...people wanted to move at different paces in their career lifecycles, and it is not the same for one individual all along. It changes according to which part of your life you are in.'[13]

Flexible arrangements that are aligned with a long-term career plan have a greater chance of retaining people. In contrast, flexible work that decreases people's possibilities by taking up more responsibilities in the future, is destined to fail.

Best practices at a glance

Globant: careers at full speed

With offices in Latin America, the US and the UK, Globant is a young but experienced offshore IT outsourcer, with customers including Google, lastminute.com, Dell, Accenture, Renault, and Citi, among others.

Being a technological firm, Globant's employees are mainly young people with an IT background. The 'Globers', as employees are called, comprise a generation that is difficult to retain. 'This generation wants to be challenged all the time. Today it is very important to have a clear career path for these young people that want to rush through the career ladder.'[14] With a philosophy of having fun while working,[15] and with a very relaxed atmosphere, every Globant office has its own distinctive atmosphere created by the office's employees (see pictures below).

The firm has designed four career paths that aim to satisfy different vocational expectations over time. The four paths are Becoming a Guru, Choose Your Own Adventure, Management Programme, and Intrapreneurship.

Becoming a Guru refers to helping people become an expert in a particular field or technology. The company provides all the training and certifications the professional needs to achieve this level of knowledge.

Choose Your Own Adventure gives employees the option to work in different areas, trying out different opportunities and shaping their own career profile.

In the Management Program, people are trained and developed to be able to take on managerial responsibilities in the future.

Finally, through the Intrepreneurship path, employees may propose an idea for the company to develop, or they can develop the idea themselves with the firm's support.

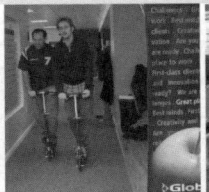

Pictures courtesy of Globant

'It is critical to have developed these paths. Our employees, all young people, want to feel they advance in what they are doing. And in an industry in which finding talent is both key and difficult, we cannot just offer a job, we need to offer a future.'[16]

5.4 THE CASE OF MANAGEMENT CONSULTING FIRMS AND THEIR RETENTION MODEL

Management consulting firms have been considered by Alvesson (2000b) as knowledge-intensive firms along with law, accounting, engineering, IT, advertising, R&D, and high-tech firms. Human capital in these firms is of strategic importance because it typically consists of individual-specific knowledge (Carvalho & Cabral-Cardoso, 2008). For instance, while a certain degree of turnover is taken to be beneficial for these companies (Baden-Fuller & Bateson, 1990), if a key person leaves, the firm may lose clients if they follow the particular individual to his or her new firm. Thus, for such firms, the risk of greatest concern is that talented employees will leave the firm, taking with them their particular knowledge.

Given the importance of human capital to the success of knowledge-intensive firms, and of management consulting firms in particular, they are interesting cases to study. These firms have the most to gain from developing talent management practices that increase retention and reinforce loyalty, and hence the talent management practices that they implement may be instructive for other firms that also seek to increase employee retention and loyalty.

Taking into account the retention framework above, let's try to understand the key factors that influence employee motivation and loyalty at management consulting companies.

The first factor is compensation. These firms generally offer above-market salaries (after the first years of an individual's career), deferred compensation plans, and retention bonuses. Each of these compensation practices is designed to motivate employees to deliver a high level of performance.

The second factor relates to career advancement. Management consulting firms often have a vertical structure with well-defined stages (i.e., junior associate, senior associate, manager, and partner). Becoming a partner is the aim of most consultants. However, to maintain a competitive environment that further incentivizes high performance, employees that do not show potential to rise to the next level are forced to exit the company. In these so-called up-or-out systems, forced rankings are commonly the basis for promote or exit decisions.

The third and final factor is social identity. For many management consulting firms, social identity associated with a particular department or project may be relevant to job satisfaction, loyalty, and hence motivation (Alvesson, 2000b).

In summary, management consulting firms endeavor to retain talented professionals by providing more money, power, and social rank relative to competing firms in the market place. Figure 5.4 summarizes these three core elements of management consulting firms' retention strategies.

Why are these three factors critical to understanding retention in management consulting firms? Imagine that these firms were to instead emphasize the importance of only two of these factors: compensation and career progression. A focus on these two factors would lead to a utilitarian view of internal relationships. Of course, a corporate identity can be created around these factors. But the resulting identity is not going to be a positive identity with potential to last. The reason is that while the compensation and partnership systems will lead to loyalty built on long-term relationships (Alvesson, 2000b), the up-or-out system that is critical to inducing high levels of performance in these companies can also strain employee relationships and, in turn, firm morale and performance. Thus, these firms must take care to also manage the social environment of the firm to avoid the negative consequences associated with a strict utilitarian view of internal relationships. This can be achieved by managing loyalty through social identification and bonding, which encourage people to feel part of the firm and also by managing exit, which can avoid a negative work environment and thereby prevent the departure of additional employees.

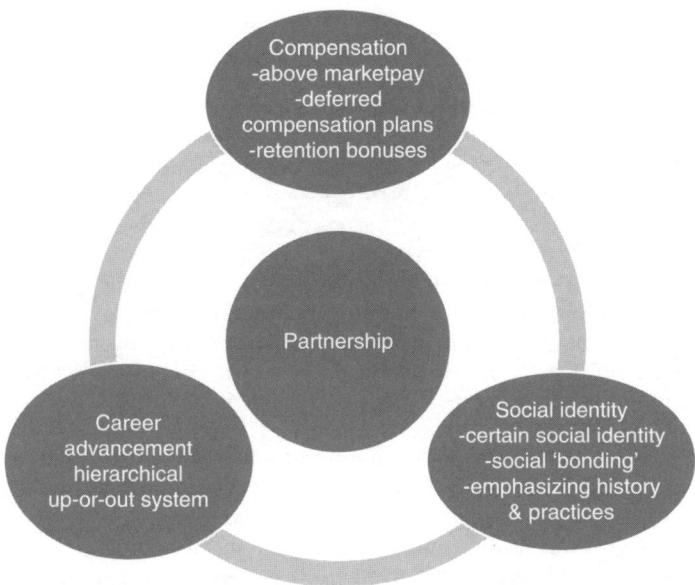

FIGURE 5.4 **Retention strategy in management consulting firms**

Off the record

Spin offs: when a retention framework fails[17]

In an article in the *Wall Street Journal*, Hilary Stout writes on the spin-off of eLoyalty from TSC, a company that has a solid reputation as a consulting and systems integration firm. The article illustrates the effect of weak employee loyalty on a company's ability to retain talent.

'Y2K contracts started to dry up a couple of years ago. At the same time, Mr. Kelly Conway's division started to boom. Mr. Conway felt stuck. The problems with ERP were hurting the entire firm. The company's stock price was slipping, and Mr. Conway was having trouble attracting the top-notch people he wanted to hire. He thought about leaving and starting his own firm, but he didn't want to engender any bad blood if he tried to take TSC employees with him. He decided his best option was to work within the structure of TSC to establish a more autonomous business.

'In September 1998, he went to John Kohler, TSC's chief executive, who agreed that something had to be done to satisfy shareholders. They brainstormed and came up with a startling plan: spin off Mr. Conway's fast-growing division into a separate company. That, they felt, would unlock shareholder value and keep impatient executives from leaving TSC. The plan

(Continued)

also fit Mr. Kohler's personal agenda. He wanted to leave TSC but didn't want to have to choose between Mr. Conway and the head of the ERP arm, whom he also liked. It all made sense. Carrying it out was another matter.

'(...) Other senior managers were eager to work for the promising new company, but Mr. Conway wasn't interested in hiring them. The problem grew once the entire 1,300-person staff was told of the impending spin off. In most cases, it was clear from the jobs they were doing where each employee would work. But a number of those pegged to TSC asked to transfer to the new firm. TSC accused Mr. Conway's group of soliciting its employees, which Mr. Conway denies. So in the summer of 1999, he stopped accepting employee transfers. "It put everybody in an impossible situation", he says.'

The spin-off of eLoyalty shows how important employee loyalty can be for a company. TSC clearly lacked a strong organizational identity that motivated talent to stay with the company. In particular, it seems that while Mr Conway's division enjoyed a strong social identity, low levels of organizational-level identity followed from a weak or unappealing corporate culture. Career opportunities outside Mr Conway's department also seemed to be insufficient to lead to strong retention motives, because many employees wanted to migrate to the new firm upon the announcement of the spin-off, that is, many employees viewed the new firm as offering better opportunities to advance their careers. The new firm also gave stock options to all employees, not just people at the vice president level or higher, as was the case at TSC. Moreover, anyone who had a TSC option automatically received an option in eLoyalty, decreasing the cost to senior talent of leaving TSC for eLoyalty. In summary, this case study shows the critical role that compensation, career advancement opportunities, and social identity can have in explaining retention.

The foregoing discussion on the three factors important to employee retention at knowledge-intensive firms, and in particular at management consulting companies, aids understanding of the dynamics behind an effective retention model. Figure 5.5 summarizes these dynamics. Preserving the equilibrium of the model is critical to achieving retention.

To summarize, an organization's retention model needs to be comprehensive. The factors above, namely, compensation, career advancement, and social identity, are each critical to a successful retention strategy. A comprehensive compensation system should include

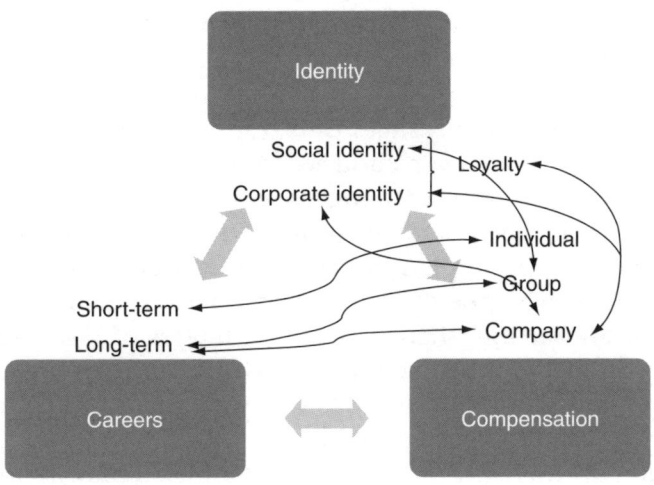

FIGURE 5.5 **The dynamics of the retention model**

individual, group, and company bonuses to incentivize individual effort while also leading employees to work productively with each other toward a common organizational purpose. Career advancement opportunities should have both short- and long-term advancement goals to motivate employees to deliver strong current performance while also developing skills that will further benefit the firm in the future. And the organization's identity should strengthen an employee's long-term bond with the firm while a strong department-level identity should further motivate performance in the current position.

The interaction of the three factors above will also contribute to the success of a retention program. A wide variety of compensation incentives (i.e., individual, group, and company) can help organizations enhance both social and organization-level identity. Short- and long-term career advancement opportunities can help companies to raise awareness of the importance of the firm's values and culture. Finally, increasing awareness of the firm's values and culture, that is, building a strong social and corporate identity, will increase employees' desire to stay with the organization for a long time. Such an identity requires a long-term perspective in terms of career advancement and compensation so that the entire system is viewed by employees to be consistent and coherent.

Organizational identity, compensation and rewards, and careers and employability are all key elements of a successful retention model. It is no longer sufficient for firms to focus their retention efforts on compensation and benefits packages only. Of course, people want to be recognized by being paid fairly and according to their performance, but aiming to recognize people through pay and benefits is short-sighted if fostering commitment and engagement are not also included in the organization's retention plan. If people are not engaged because they are not satisfied with the direction their career is taking or the experience they are having, then it is only a matter of time before they will leave. Similarly, if people do not identify with the organization's core values and as a result do not fit in with the firm's culture, their commitment can be expected to suffer.

Retention is therefore much more complex today than it once was. This means that in building their retention plan, firms need to make sure there is coherence between the organization's values, individuals' career paths, and the compensation and rewards system. The more coherent this model is, the higher the chances are of a committed, engaged, and recognized workforce, and hence the more likely that retention will increase. Table 5.1 summarizes the key differences between the old retention paradigms and retention strategies appropriate for the talent mess era.

'Total rewards programs' are an attempt to gather together the different elements of our retention model. Therefore, a complete

TABLE 5.1 **Retention over time**

Old retention paradigms	New retention strategies
Compensation and benefits packages are the focus of the retention strategy	Compensation and rewards, career paths and organizational identity are all the focus of the retention strategy
Retention focus is short term	Retention focus is long term; requires a coherent model in which organizational values, career paths and reward systems are connected
Focus of careers: employment and climbing the career ladder	Focus of careers: employability and flexible career paths
Organizational values are explained in the company's mission	Commitment and engagement with the firm's culture and values are key issues for retention

reward strategy should include wages, benefits, career paths, and work environment. Aselstine and Alletson (2006) agree with this framework but also include learning and development. They state that an organization's total rewards strategy should reinforce the human capital strategy. A good example of this can be found at Dow Chemical, which successfully introduced a total rewards program that not only improved the company's compensation practices, but also went beyond compensation in implementing a retention strategy.

CASE IN POINT: DOW

Dow: total rewards

The Dow Chemical Company was founded in 1897 by Herbert H. Dow to manufacture and sell bleach on a commercial scale. Since then, Dow has become a diversified chemical company with annual sales of US$ 57.5 bn and 46,000 employees worldwide. The company delivers a broad range of products and services in 160 countries, accounting for 46,000 employees worldwide.[18]

At Dow, the concept of Total Rewards supersedes the idea of compensation. Total Rewards describes the entire portfolio of offerings the company provides to its employees. As the Global Compensation Leader noted, 'Total Rewards encompasses not just paying benefits, but also the culture and work environment offered by the company to all our employees across the globe.'[19]

Dow's concept of Total Rewards includes the following features: culture and principles; pay; recognition; benefits; learning and development; health; time off; and career planning.

Pay and benefits at Dow are competitive in relation to the best of the companies against which it competes for talent and are tailored to each country so as to take into account local tax structures. Further, they reflect both employee and company performance. For instance, Dow encourages stock ownership among all employees, as it is regarded as a useful way to align employee efforts with company stock performance. The plan allows employees to purchase shares of common stock through payroll deductions or through lump sum payments during a specified time period. This incentive is quite popular, with 48% of the firm's employees worldwide subscribed to this program in 2007. However, the global stock program is not just a question of incentives for top managers: 'Long-term incentives are, in some cases, mechanisms of retention. But for top managers this is part of their compensation package and it needs to be competitive when compared to the market.'[20]

Recognition at Dow is also very important, as the company emphasizes building a 'people-centric performance culture'.[21] Dow has implemented a recognition program that can be used by all Dow employees to show their appreciation in a timely and direct manner. In particular, through a web-based system, employees can send a thank you, electronic gift certificates (from one to three carats) or a diamond keepsake cash award for up to 30% of their monthly salary that is delivered through payroll. In 2006, more than 125,000 awards were submitted, and each year the firm has spent between US$16 and US$20 m on recognition.[22]

Career plans are also taken into account in the Total Rewards program. As a global company, the development possibilities are

FIGURE 5.6 **Recognition at Dow**
Used with permission

high, so the pace at which the employee wants his or her career to go is seriously considered. For instance, as the HR Director of the Basic Chemicals Business Group notes, 'There are some people who would prefer a global career, others that would rather stay in their country. Dow always tries to find opportunities aligned with people's interests.'[23] Similarly, the Global Director of Compensation and Benefits observes: 'When you go around the room and ask why it is that you like to work at Dow, people always mention "Well, I like the fact that I've had multiple careers within this company: I started off as an engineer, and I've worked in Purchasing, and now I'm working in Human Resources" or "I've lived in different locations, I've worked in different areas".'[24]

Interestingly, Dow's Total Rewards philosophy extends beyond the standard practices of a Total Rewards package. For instance, Dow supports flexible work schedules (either telecommuting or time flexibility), and provides numerous learning and development opportunities. Dow is also committed to environmental issues in communities where it is located and encourages healthy lifestyles (e.g., 'no tobacco day', 'take a walk day', and other company-wide health-related events). And these are only a few of the offerings of the Total Rewards program. As the HR Director of the Basic Chemicals Group observes: 'Today's young professionals are interested in the environment, and in the way we as organizations commit to the community, among others. They want to feel proud of the organization they are working in.'[25] Figure 5.7 illustrates the scope of Dow's Total Rewards program.[26]

'To think of Total Rewards and people's experiences, think of a palette. Think of a painter's palette, and on this palette, he has the green colour, the blue colour, the yellow colour, and the orange colour. And all of these colours are available to the painter during the process of painting, and, when you're brand new in your career, what matters most to you are some of the things that you find in the "My Experience at Dow". But then, when you get to 20 years within the company there are other things that become more important to you from a career perspective.'[27]

In summary, Dow offers its employees an opportunity to create their own experiences. They can get access, through the intranet, to all available offerings and proposals, and they can create their own experiences from the portfolio of Total Rewards available to them.

The challenges for the future of the Total Rewards program are clear for those responsible for implementing the system: 'At least for the

FIGURE 5.7 **Total Rewards at Dow**

next couple of years, our biggest challenge is to make some tough calls that we need to make to come out of this (economic) crisis.[28] So, some of the elements of Total Rewards may not be perceived by employees during this crisis. But I think our biggest challenge is to continue to do the right thing and continue to push Total Rewards, even during these tough times, so that when we finally come out, employees see the value of the systems and working for Dow.'[29]

CHAPTER HIGHLIGHTS

❖ Retaining talent requires long-term thinking to avoid short-sighted perspectives.

❖ The framework for thinking about retention strategically has three components:

  ■ Organizational identity, which increases commitment
  ■ Compensation and rewards, which increase recognition
  ■ Career paths and employability, which increase engagement.

❖ Commitment, recognition, and employability are all necessary to increase retention.

❖ A strong organizational identity that is rooted in values that are central, distinctive, and enduring helps the employee identity with the company, increasing the employee's commitment.

❖ Compensation and rewards increase retention by recognizing people for performance. Compensation and rewards should be flexible, so that they can be adapted to different types of people within an organization. Moreover, it is important to compensate employees on an individual as well as a group basis, to effectively incentivize retention and performance.

❖ Retention also requires engagement, which is fostered by providing employees with opportunities to learn and develop. As the idea of a job for life is fading, transforming the job market requires organizations to change their mindset, increasing one's employability along an ever-changing career path.

VERY IMPORTANT QUESTIONS

☙ What are the main dimensions considered by your organization when thinking about a retention strategy?

☙ Does your firm convey the importance of the organization's identity and values to its employees?

☙ Does your organization have deeply rooted values, or are its values changing frequently?

☙ Are your firm's actions consistent with the values it communicates?

☙ Is your firm's career model rooted in a hierarchical path? Or does it offer different options depending on individuals' needs and career stages?

☙ What is the strategy for career advancement for those in a talent pool?

☙ Does your firm's compensation strategy contain short- and long-term incentives?

☙ Does your firm support performance-related pay at different levels?

6

CONNECTING THE DOTS: ATTRACTION, DEVELOPMENT, AND RETENTION

The last three chapters have separately analyzed the three main dimensions of talent management: attraction, development, and retention. By looking at these dimensions separately, it is possible to discuss the nuances and complexity of each. However, it would be a mistake to end the analysis without explaining how the different elements of talent management are connected.

Many companies consider talent management to be a linear process in which attraction, development, and retention are distinct. But often these companies find that a lack of connections between these different areas makes the entire process internally inconsistent and, hence, poorly aligned with the firm's overall business strategy. Other organizations focus only on attracting and retaining people, but overlook the critical process of development. These companies tend to find themselves prisoners of short-term practices and policies.

For a talent management strategy to be successful, it should be treated as a process in which attraction, development, and retention are all interrelated. While each dimension has its own particular features, their co-ordinated interaction is critical for the coherence of the entire process, and hence for the performance of the firm.

Figure 6.1 illustrates a talent management model in which the areas of attraction, development, and retention are interrelated.

In Figure 6.1, 'align', or the connection between attraction and development, refers to the ability of a firm to support a strategy by orienting an organization's people, practices, and processes with the

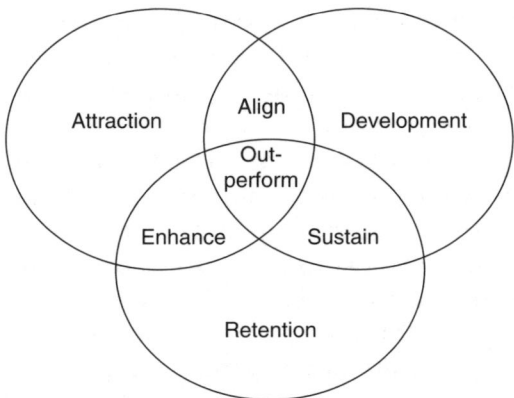

FIGURE 6.1 **A talent management model**

accomplishment of strategic issues. Important questions that need to be addressed to achieve alignment include:

- Do new employee programs link newcomers with the company's current reality?
- Does the organization fulfil its employees' expectations, that is, do development programs maintain the firm's 'attractiveness' (e.g., by segmenting the programs so that each generation feels connected to the company)?
- Are development programs aligned with the business strategy?

'Sustain', or the connection between development and retention, refers to the ability of organizations to maintain a long-term relationship with their employees. The role of employee development is critical to sustaining a long-term relationship, as organizations that offer continued learning offer not only employment, but also employability, which makes staying at the company more desirable. Some questions that need to be addressed to ensure that a company can consistently 'sustain' long-term relationships with its employees include:

- Do employees have a chance to learn and hone new skills through various types of learning opportunities?
- Is the company offering employees opportunities to develop their careers?

To reiterate earlier discussions, to sustain a long-term relationship with employees, organizations must look at new paradigms in terms of development. Organizational silos that impede the ability of people to move within the firm should be avoided in favor of talent pools and greater intra-organizational mobility so that employees can grow from a larger and more varied set of development opportunities.

'Enhance', or the connection between attraction and retention, refers to the ability of organizations to boost both attraction and retention through values and actions that enhance the desirability of working and staying with the company. For instance, while the EVP needs to convey a clear message to attract prospective employees, this message will have an impact on the commitment of those already working with the company. Thus, the company's external image and internal organizational identity are closely linked. Similarly, while a flexible, merit-based rewards system can be an important tool to retain people at different stages of their lives and careers, it is also a factor that is important in attracting talent to the firm. A strong organizational identity also works to both attract and retain talent. To be able to 'enhance', the following questions should be addressed:

- What elements of the EVP are critical for both attracting and retaining talent?
- Does the organization's identity forge a strong and coherent culture that connects people to the company? Does this organizational identity enjoy a certain prestige within the market?
- Is the rewards system fair, competitive, and tied to performance?

Finally, 'out-perform', or the area in which attraction, development, and retention all overlap, refers to the ability of a firm to deliver a holistic talent management strategy that supports the overall business strategy and, in turn, allows the firm to achieve a strong performance in the market. Figure 6.2 captures how integrating attraction, development, and retention can lead to out-performance by creating a dynamic model of talent management.

Above it is suggested that aligning the talent management strategy with the business strategy requires that the three areas of talent management (i.e., attraction, development, and retention) be tightly integrated. This means that an organization has a single, coherent plan that brings each of these areas all together. Such coherence is achieved through consistency across the different areas. A focus on consistency

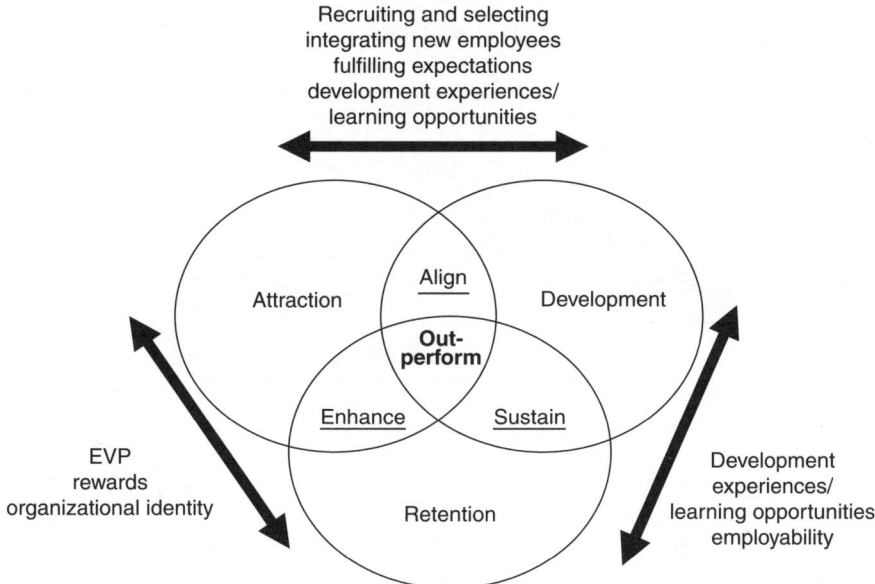

FIGURE 6.2 **A dynamic model of talent management**

should begin with human resources, which should implement a well-thought-out set of processes and practices that reinforce each other across the different stages of the talent management process. Baron & Kreps (1999, p. 57) specify important forms of consistency in this regard: 'Consistency between HR practices and current initiatives in business strategy and technology; consistency of HR practices with one another; consistency in practices across (at least similar) employees, and consistency or continuity between HR practices in the past, present and future.' By achieving consistency, the company will send a clear and reliable message to employees, resulting in improved employee attitudes and behaviors and, in turn, better communication with employees (Baron & Kreps, 1999) and greater trust. Figure 6.3 shows how the talent management model depicted in Figure 6.2 leads to consistency and coherence, and hence alignment with the overall business strategy.

The above point is emphasized by Stahl et al. (2007), who study the talent management practices of 37 multinationals. In particular, these authors show that those companies that excel at talent management ensure internal consistency, complementarity, and reinforcement of

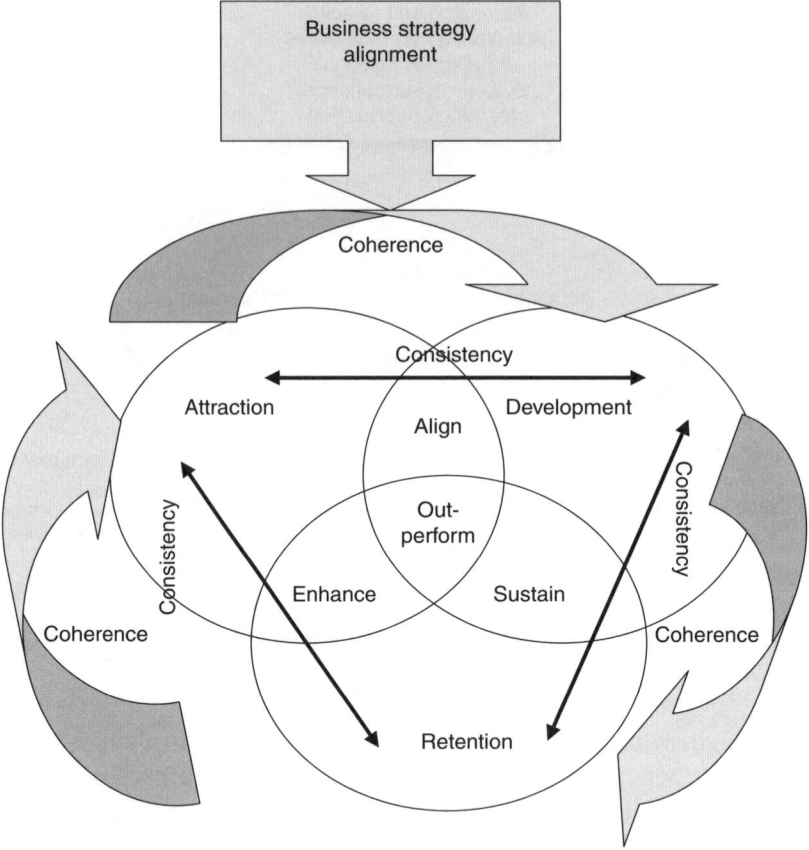

FIGURE 6.3 **Consistency and coherence in a talent management model**

the practices implemented to attract, develop, and retain talent. More-over, the authors show that a focus on consistency helps these firms align talent management with the corporate culture, business strategy, and long-term goals of the organization. Thus, the authors suggest that competitive advantage comes not simply from designing and imple-menting best practices ('companies around the world are becoming more similar – and more sophisticated – in their recruitment, develop-ment, measurement, and management of high potential employees'), but rather from internal alignment of talent management practices and the firm's value system and strategy.

In contrast, inconsistency across talent management areas can lead to organizational schizophrenia, which reduces trust in the talent management program and ultimately can be fatal to the success of the entire talent management model (Becker et al., 1997). Examples of inconsistency abound. Just think of firms that hire consultants, host outdoor activities, and develop a variety of workshops in an effort to facilitate teamwork but that limit pay rises or other rewards to individual performance. Such inconsistencies put the effectiveness of the entire talent management program at risk. Fortunately, by designing a consistent, coherent talent management model, it can be easily aligned with the business strategy. In effect, the talent management process would thus become strategic in its own right.

NOTES

CHAPTER 1

1 Baby Boomers refers to the post-war generation (1946–64). Generation X refers to people born between 1965 and 1980. Generation Y includes those born between 1981 and 1995. Finally, Generation Z comprises those people born after 1995 still not in the labor market (Guthridge et al., 2008; Terjesen & Viola Frey, 2008).

2 CIPD (2006c).

3 Heidrick & Struggles (2007).

4 Friedman et al. (2008).

CHAPTER 2

1 CIPD (2006a).

2 CIPD (2006b).

3 CIPD (2006c).

4 Rosas, close to the French border in the north-east of Spain, is the closest town to Cala Montjoi, where elBulli is established.

5 Adrià et al. (2008).

6 The Michelin Guide is the industry reference for assessing the best restaurants worldwide. Three Michelin stars is the maximum award given by Michelin, indicating exceptional cuisine.

7 Interview with Ferran Adrià, co-owner of elBulli restaurant, Rosas, Spain.

8 Interview with Ferran Adrià, co-owner of elBulli restaurant, Rosas, Spain.

9 Interview with Juli Soler, co-owner of elBulli restaurant, Rosas, Spain.

10 Adrià et al. (2008).

11 elBulli has co-branding agreements with firms such as NH Hotels, Nestlé, Borges (food manufacturer), and Lavazza (coffee).

12 Interview with Alejandro Digilio, chef and ex-stager at elBulli.

CHAPTER 3

1   <http://careers.jnj.com/careers/global/index.htm> (accessed May 18, 2010).

2   <http://www.mckinsey.com/careers/who_is_mckinsey/what_makes_us_different. aspx> (accessed May 18, 2010).

3   Four companies are part of the Royal Mail Group: Royal Mail, Post Office, Parcelforce Worldwide, and General Logistics Systems (GLS).

4   Source of information: Graduate Program brochure, Royal Mail.

5   Interview with Head of Resourcing, Royal Mail, London.

6   Extracted from http://www.vault.com.

7   <http://www.southwest.com/about_swa/press/factsheet.html (accessed May 18, 2010).

8   Southwest Airlines 2008 Annual Report.

9   <http://www.southwest.com/careers/benefits.html> (accessed May 18, 2010).

10   Frauenheim (2008).

11   Gary Kelly, CEO, Southwest Airlines.

12   'Generation Y Goes to Work' (2008). *The Economist* print edition. December 30.

13   As heard in a conference by Lynn Heward in reference to casting and training. Lynn is the former president and CEO of *Cirque du Soleil's* Creative Content Division and is currently executive producer for a variety of special projects. The author wants to thank *Cirque du Soleil* for cross-checking the information in this section and for allowing the use of the company's logo.

14   <http://www.cirquedusoleil.com> (accessed May 18, 2010).

15   <http://www.cirquedusoleil.com> (accessed May 18, 2010).

16   <http://www.cirquedusoleil.com/en/about/intro/intro.asp> (accessed May 18, 2010).

17   Belkin (2007).

18   <http://www.google.com/support/jobs/bin/static.py?page=benefits.html> (accessed May 18, 2010).

19   <http://nyjobsource.com/google.html> (accessed May 18, 2010).

20   <http://www.pg.com/jobs/sectionmain.shtml> (accessed May 18, 2010).

21   Friedman et al. (2008).

22   Information provided by the company.

23   Second Life caters for users who are over 18 years old. Teen Second Life is restricted to users who are between 13 and 18 years old.

24   Covel (2007).

25   O'Reilly & Pfeffer (1996).

26   DeLong & Vijayaraghavan (2002).

27   Thompson (2004).

28 Interview with General Manager, Hotel Faena+Universe, Buenos Aires, Argentina.

29 Interview with Training Manager, Hotel Faena+Universe, Buenos Aires, Argentina.

30 Interview with General Manager, Faena Hotel+Universe, Buenos Aires, Argentina.

31 <http://www.loreal.com/_en/_ww/html/our-company/facts-figures.aspx?> (accessed May 18, 2010).

32 Interview with Executive Vice President of Human Resources, L'Oréal, Paris.

33 Used with the company's permission.

34 Used with the company's permission.

35 Interview with International Co-ordinator for Corporate Communication, L'Oréal, Paris.

36 Interview with International Recruitment Development Director, L'Oréal, Paris.

37 Interview with Recruitment Manager for Cosmetics, L'Oréal, Paris.

38 Interview with Executive Vice President of Human Resources, L'Oréal, Paris.

39 Used with the company's permission.

40 Interview with International Recruitment Development Director, L'Oréal, Paris.

41 Sources: L' Oréal Annual Report, L'Oréal's FIT brochure, interviews.

42 Interview with International Recruitment Development Director, L'Oréal, Paris.

CHAPTER 4

1 Marquez (2007).

2 <http://www.puig.com/#/en_GB/brands-products.prestige-brands> (accessed May 18, 2010).

3 <http://www.puig.com/#/en_GB/people.work-with-us> (accessed May 18, 2010).

4 Interview with Chief of Human Resources and Chief Legal Officer at Puig, Barcelona.

5 Interview with Talent Project – Corporate HR at Puig, Barcelona.

6 Interview with Talent Project – Corporate HR at Puig, Barcelona.

7 Interview with Global Leadership and Talent Development Manager, BAT, London.

8 Gladwell (2002).

9 Strategic agility refers to the ability to think conceptually and to handle complexity. Emotional agility refers to the ability of someone to harness their emotions and influence others. Learning agility refers to the ability to stretch one's boundaries or learn.

10 Interview with Head of Leadership Development, Royal Mail, London.

11 Interview with Learning and Developing Manager, Lastminute.com, London.

12 <http://www.pfizer.com/about/leadership_and_structure/company_fact_sheet.jsp> (accessed May 18, 2010).

13 Interview with Performance Management Leader, Pfizer.

14 Interview with Performance Management Leader, Pfizer.

15 Interview with Performance Management Leader, Pfizer.

16 The 80/20 Rule means that in most cases, 80% of the results are due to 20% of the causes, or that only a few (20%) of the causes are vital whereas many (80%) are trivial. In Pareto's case, he observed that 20% of the people owned 80% of the wealth.

17 Smedley (2007).

18 Norwich Union (2007).

19 For more information on implementing the strength-based approach, contact the Centre for Applied Positive Psychology. See http://www.cappeu.org/.

20 Figure based on Berke et al. (2008).

21 These are the sources to build a list for development methods: Berke et al. (2008); Van Dam (2007); Rothwell & Kazanas (2003); Michaels et al. (2001).

22 Interview with Head of Leadership Development, Royal Mail, London.

23 <http://www.deloitte.com/dtt/press_release/0,1014,sid%253D1018%2526cid %253D217344,00.html> (accessed May 18, 2010).

24 Interview with Dr. Nick Van Dam, Global Director for Learning for Deloitte Touche Tohmatsu and Director Human Capital for Deloitte Consulting.

25 Interview with Dr. Nick Van Dam, Deloitte Touche Tohmatsu, Amsterdam.

26 <http://www.syngenta.com/en/about_syngenta/companyhistory.html> (accessed May 18, 2010).

27 Used with permission.

28 Used with permission.

29 Koelbing & Frei.

30 Interview with Head Strategic Projects Talent Management, Syngenta, Basel.

31 Leader Development Guide. Information provided by Syngenta, Basel.

32 Leader Development Guide. Information provided by Syngenta, Basel.

33 Leader Development Guide. Information provided by Syngenta, Basel.

CHAPTER 5

1 Tower Perrin (2008).

2 Interview with AGD Director, Buenos Aires, Argentina.

3 Tower Perrin (2008).

4 Bimbo: Una historia para creer y crear. Sesenta aniversario 1945–2005. Edición Grupo Bimbo. <http://www.grupobimbo.com> (accessed May 18, 2010).

5 <http://www.grupobimbo.com/display.php?section=1&subsection=26> (accessed May 18, 2010).

6 Servitje (2003).

7 Interview with Organizational Development Manager, Latam Bimbo.

8 For the British version, refer to: <http://www.bbc.co.uk/comedy/theoffice>. For the American version, refer to: <http://www.nbc.com/The_Office> (accessed May 18, 2010).

9 Marquez (2008).

10 Interview with Learning and Development Manager, Human Resources, AON, London.

11 Interview with Executive Vice President Human Resources, L'Oréal, Paris.

12 Interview with Global Leadership and Talent Development Manager, BAT, London.

13 Interview with Global Leadership and Talent Development Manager, BAT, London.

14 Interview with Career and Talent Development Manager, Globant.

15 <http://www.globant.com/Content/Having_Fun/Pictures_Of_Our_Offices/index.html> (accessed May 18, 2010).

16 Interview with Career and Talent Development Manager, Globant.

17 Stout (2000).

18 <http://www.dow.com/about/> (accessed May 18, 2010).

19 Interview with Global Compensation Leader, Dow, Midland, USA.

20 Interview with HR Director, Basic Chemicals Business Group, Dow, Midland, USA.

21 <http://www.dow.com/about/aboutdow/vision.htm> (accessed May 18, 2010).

22 Company's information.

23 Interview with HR Director, Basic Chemicals Business Group, Dow, Midland, USA.

24 Interview with Global Director, Compensation and Benefits, Dow, Midland, USA.

25 Interview with HR Director, Basic Chemicals Business Group, Dow, Midland, USA.

26 Used with permission.

27 Interview with Global Director, Compensation and Benefits, Dow, Midland, USA.

28 The global financial and economic crisis of 2008.

29 Interview with Global Compensation Leader, Dow, Midland, USA.

BIBLIOGRAPHY

Adrià, F., Adrià, A., & Soler, J. (2008). *A Day at elBulli: An Insight into the Ideas, Methods and Creativity of Ferran Adrià*. London: Phaidon Press.

Albert, S. & Whetten, D. A. (1985). 'Organizational identity', in L. L. Cummings & B. M. Staw (eds.), *Research in Organizational Behaviour*, vol. 7, pp. 263–95. Greenwich, CT: JAI Press.

Alsop, R. (2008). *The Trophy Kids Grow Up: How the Millennial Generation is Shaking Up the Workplace*. San Francisco, CA: Jossey-Bass.

Alvesson, M. (1987). 'Organizations, culture, and ideology'. *International Studies of Management and Organization* 17(3): 4.

Alvesson, M. (2000a). 'The local and the grandiose: method, micro and macro in comparative studies of culture and organizations', in R. Tzeng & B. Uzzi (eds.), *Embeddedness and Corporate Change in a Global Economy*. New York: Peter Lang.

Alvesson, M. (2000b). 'Social identity and the problem of loyalty in knowledge-intensive companies'. *Journal of Management Studies* 37(8): 1101–23.

Aselstine, K. & Alletson, K. (2006). 'A new deal for the 21st century workplace'. *Ivey Business Journal*, March/April, 1–7.

Baden-Fuller, C. & Bateson, J. (1990). 'Promotion strategies for hierarchically organised professional service firms: is up or out always the best?'. *International Journal of Service Industry Management* 1(3): 62–78.

Barner, R. (2006). *Bench Strength*. New York: Amacom.

Barney, J. (1991). 'Firm resources and sustained competitive advantage'. *Journal of Management* 17(1): 99–120.

Barney, J. (1995). 'Looking inside for competitive advantage'. *Academy of Management Executive* 9(4): 49–61.

Baron, J. N., Burton, M. D., & Hannan, M. T. (1996). 'The road taken: the origins and evolution of employment systems in high-tech firms'. *Industrial and Corporate Change* 5(2): 239–75.

Baron, J. N. & Kreps, D. M. (1999). *Strategic Human Resources*. New York: Wiley & Son.

Becker, B. E., Huselid, M. A., Pickus, P. S., & Spratt, M. F. (1997). 'HR as a source of shareholder value: research and recommendations'. *Human Resource Management* 36(1): 39–47.

Beechler, S. & Woodward, I. C. (2009). 'The global "war for talent" '. *Journal of International Management* 15: 273–85.

Belkin, D. (2007). 'Talent scouts for Cirque du Soleil walk a tightrope'. *Wall Street Journal*, September 8.

Benko, C. & Weisberg, A. (2007). *Mass Career Customization*. Boston: Harvard Business School Press.

Berke, D., Kossler, M. E., & Wakefield, M. (2008). *Developing Leadership Talent*. San Francisco: Pfeiffer.

Bowers, D., & Kleiner, B. H. (2005). 'Behavioral Interviewing'. *Management Research News* 28(11–12): 107–14.

Boudreau, J. W. & Ramstad, P. M. (2005). 'Talentship and the new paradigm for human resource management: from professional practice to strategic talent decision science'. *Human Resource Planning* 28(2): 17–26.

Branham, L. (2001). *Keeping the People Who Keep You in Business*. New York: Amacom.

Brown, P. & Hesketh, A. (2004). *The Mismanagement of Talent*. Oxford: Oxford University Press.

Byham, W. C., Smith, A. B., & Paese, M. J. (2002). *Grow Your Own Leaders: How to Identify, Develop, and Retain Leadership Talent*. New York: FT Press.

Capelli, P. (1999). *The New Deal at Work*. Boston: Harvard Business School Press.

Capelli, P. (2008a). 'Talent management for the twenty-first century'. *Harvard Business Review*, March issue.

Capelli, P. (2008b). *Talent on Demand*. Boston: Harvard Business School Press.

Carvalho, A. & Cabral-Cardoso, C. (2008). 'Flexibility through HRM in management consulting firms'. *Personnel Review* 37(3): 332–49.

Cheese, P., Thomas, R., & Craig, E. (2008). *The Talent Powered Organization*. London: Kogan Page.

Child, J. (2005). *Organization: Contemporary Principles and Practices*. Oxford: Blackwell Publishing.

CIPD (2006a). *Learning and Development*. London: Chartered Institute of Personnel and Development.

CIPD (2006b). *Reflections on Talent Management*. London: Chartered Institute of Personnel and Development.

CIPD (2006c). *Talent Management: Understanding the Dimensions*. London: Chartered Institute of Personnel and Development.

Clifford, S., Scudamore, B., Blumberg, J., & Levine, A. (2006). 'The new science of hiring'. *Inc. Magazine*, August issue, 90–8.

Cohen, D. S. (2001). *The Talent Edge*. Ontario: John Wiley & Sons.

Collings, D. G. & Mellahi, K. (2009). 'Strategic talent management: a review and research agenda'. *Human Resource Management Review* 19: 204–313.

Collins, J. C. & Porras, J. I. (2000). *Built to Last*. Great Britain: Random House Business Books.

Colvin, G. (2008). *Talent is Overrated*. New York: Portfolio (Penguin Group).

Covel, S. (2007). 'Start-up lures talent with creative pitch'. *Wall Street Journal*, June 3.

Coyle, D. (2009). *The Talent Code: Greatness Isn't Born. It's Grown. Here is How*. New York: Bantam Dell.

Cross, R., Baker, W., & Parker, A. (2003). 'What creates energy in organizations?'. *MITSloan Management Review* 44(4): 51–6.

D'Aveni, R. A. (1994). *Hyper-Competition*. New York: The Free Press.

Davis, T., Cutt, M., Flynn, N., Mowl, P., & Orme, S. (2007). *Talent Assessment*. Hampshire: Gower Publishing.

DeLong, T. J. & Vijayaraghavan, V. (2002). *Cirque du Soleil*. Case study of Harvard Business School, University of Harvard.

Dutton, J. E. & Penner, W. J. (1993). *The Importance of Organizational Identity for Strategic Agenda Building*. Chichester: John Wiley & Sons.

Economist Intelligence Unit (2006). *The CEO's Role in Talent Management: How Top Executives from Ten Countries are Nurturing the Leaders of Tomorrow*. London: The Economist.

Eisenhardt, K. & Schoonhoven, C. B. (1990). 'Organizational growth: linking founding team, strategy, environment, and growth among U.S: semiconductor ventures, 1978–1988'. *Administrative Science Quarterly* 35: 504–29.

Figueiredo, R., & Hatum, A. (2004). *Dirigiendo Personas*. Buenos Aires: Temas Grupo Editorial.

Frank, F. D., Finnegan, R. P., & Taylor, C. R. (2004). 'The race for talent. Retaining and engaging workers in the 21st century'. *Human Resource Planning* 27(3): 12–25.

Frauenheim, E. (2008). 'Libby's Life in HR—So Far (Interview with Libby Sartain)'. *Workforce Management* 87(9) (May): 20.

Freiberg, K. & Freiberg, J. (1998). *Nuts! Southwest Airlines' Crazy Recipe for Business and Personal Success*. New York: Broadway Books.

Freidman, D., Hemerling, J., & Chapman, J. (2008). *Achieving a Global Talent Advantage*. Boston Consulting Group.

Fulmer, R. M. & Bleak, J. L. (2008). *The Leadership Advantage: How the Best Companies are Developing their Talent to Pave the Way for Future Success*. New York: Amacom.

Gagliardi, P. (1986). 'The creation and change of organizational cultures: a conceptual framework'. *Organisation Studies* 7(2): 117–34.

Gay, M. & Sims, D. (2006). *Building Tomorrow's Talent*. Milton Keynes: AuthorHouse.

Gioia, D. A. & Thomas, J. B. (1996). 'Identity, image, and issue interpretation: sensemaking during strategic change in academia'. *Administrative Science Quarterly* 41(3): 370–403.

Gladwell, M. (2002). 'The talent myth. Are smart people overrated?'. *The New Yorker*. July 22.

Gladwell, M. (2008). *Outliers: the Story of Success*. New York: Little, Brown and Company.

Goldman, S. L., Nagel, R. N., and Preiss, K. (1995). *Agile Competitors and Virtual Organizations*. New York: Van Nostrand Reinhold.

Goleman, D. (1995). *Emotional Intelligence: Why it Can Matter More than IQ*. New York: Bantam Books.

Goranson, H. T. (1999). *The Agile Virtual Enterprise*. Westport, CT: Quorum Books.

Greenwood, R. & Hinnings, C. R. (1988). 'Organizational design types, tracks and the dynamics of strategic change'.*Organization Science* 9(3): 293–316.

Grigoryev, P. (2006). 'Hiring by competency model'. *The Journal for Quality & Participation* (Winter issue): 16–18.

Grinyer, P. H., Mayer, D. H., & McKieran, P. (1988). *Sharpbenders: The Secrets of Unleashing Corporate Potential*. Oxford: Basil Blackwell.

Groysberg, B., McLean, A., & Nohria, N. (2006). 'Are leaders portable?'. *Harvard Business Review* (May 1): 1–10.

Groysberg, B., Nanda, A., & Nohria, N. (2004). 'The risky business of hiring stars'. *Harvard Business Review* (May 1): 1–10.

Gustafson, L. T. & Reger, R. K. (1995). 'Using organizational identity to achieve stability and change in high velocity environments'. *Best Papers Proceedings Academy of Management Journal*.

Guthridge, M., Komn, A. B., Lawson, E. (2008). 'Making talent a strategic priority', in *The McKinsey Quarterly* 1: 49–59.

Haeckel, S. H. (1999). 'Organizational innovation and organizational change'. *Annual Review of Sociology* 25: 597–622.

Hambrick, D. C. & Mason, P. A. (1984). 'Upper echelons: the organization as a reflection of its top managers'. *Academy of Management Review* 9(2): 193–206.

Hammonds, K. H. (2005). 'Why we hate HR'. *Fast Company* 97 (August).

Handy, C. (1996). *Beyond Certainty: The Changing Worlds of Organizations*. Boston: Harvard Business School Press.

Hatch, M. J. (1997). *Organization Theory: Modern, Symbolic and Postmodern Perspectives*. Oxford: Oxford University Press.

Hatum, A., & Pettigrew, A. M. (2006). 'Determinants of organizational flexibility: a study in an emerging economy'. *British Journal of Management* 17: 115–37.

Hatum, A. (2007). *Adaptation or Expiration in Family Firms: Organizational Flexibility in Emerging Economies*. Cheltenham: Edward Elgar.

Hatum, A., Silvestri, L., & Vassolo, R. (2008). 'Organizational identity as an anchor for adaptation: an emerging market perspective'. Organizational Identity and Ideology, paper session sponsored by the ODC division (Organizational Development and Change). Academy of Management Annual Meeting, Anaheim, California.

Hedlund, G. (1994). 'A model of knowledge management and the N-form corporation'. *Strategic Management Journal* 15: 73–90.

Heidrick & Struggles (2007). *Mapping Global Talents. Essays and Insights*. London: Economist Intelligence Unit. Available at <http://heidrick.com> (accessed May 17, 2010).

Heinen, J. S. & O'Neill, C. (2004). 'Managing talent to maximise performance'. *Employment Relations Today* 32(2): 67–82.

Heward, L., & Bacon, J. U. (2006). *The Spark: Igniting the Creative Fire That Lives With Us All*. New York: Doubleday.

Hieronimus, F., Scaefer, K., & Scchröder, J. (2005). 'Using branding to attract talent'. *The McKinsey Quarterly* 3: 12–4.

Kermally, S. (2004). *Developing and Managing Talent*. London: Thorogood.

Kim, W. C. & Mauborgne, R. (2005). *Blue Ocean Strategy*. Boston: Harvard Business Review Press.

Koelbing, C. & Frei, B. 'Smashing silos to build a fully integrated talent management process'. Presentation: Syngenta, Basel, Switzerland.

Lawler III, E. E. (2008). *Talent: Making People Your Competitive Advantage*. San Francisco: Jossey-Bass.

Levison, H. (1978). 'Abrasive personality'. *Harvard Business Review* (May–June): 86–92.

Lewis, R. E. & Heckman, R. J. (2006). 'Talent management: a critical review'. *Human Resource Management Review* 16: 139–54.

Lombardo, M. M. & Eichinger, R. W. (2000). 'High potentials as high learners'. *Human Resource Management* 39(4): 321–29.

March, J. G. (1995). 'The future, disposable organizations and the rigidities of imagination'. *Organization* 2(3–4): 427–40.

Marquez, J. (2007). 'GE's people power: Coato made jack Welch a Believer'. *Workforce Management*: 26–30.

Marquez, J. (2008). 'Jellies: Where workers' ideas come together'. *Workforce Management* (October 6): 8.

Martin, G., Beaumont, P., Doig, R., & Pate, J. (2005). 'Branding: new performance discourse for HR?'. *European Management Journal* 23(I): 76–88.

Mascarenhas, B. (2009). 'The emerging CEO agenda'. *Journal of International Management* (15): 245–50.

Michaels, E., Handfield-Jones, H. & Axelrod, B. (2001). *The War for Talent*. Boston, MA: Harvard Business School Press.

Moret, X. (2007). *elBulli Desde Dentro*. Barcelona: RBA Libros, S. A.

'Norwich Union changes focus from competencies to strengths' (2007). *Strategic HR Review* 7(1).

O'Reilly, C. & Pfeffer, J. (1996). *Southwest Airlines (A)*. Case study of the Graduate School of Business, Stamford University.

Pettigrew, A. (1979). 'On studying organizational cultures'. *Administrative Science Quarterly* 24(4): 570–81.

Pettigrew, A. M. & Fenton, E. M. (2000). *The Innovating Organization*. London: Sage Publications.

Pettigrew, A. M., Whittington, R., Melin, L., Sánchez Runde, C., van den Bosch, F. A. J., Ruigrok, W., & Numagami, T. (2003). *Innovative Forms of Organizing, International Perspectives*. London: Sage Publications.

Philbrick, J., Barbara, D. B., & Hass, M. H. (1999). 'Pre-employment screening: a decade of change'. *American Business Review* 17(2): 75–86.

Robertson, A. & Abbey, G. (2003). *Managing Talented People*. Harlow: Pearson Education Limited.

Rothwell, W. J. & Kazanas, H. C. (2004). The Strategic Development of Talent. Amherst, MA: HRD Press.

Rueff, R. & Stringer, H. (2006). *Talent Force: A New Manifesto for the Human Side of Business*. Upper Saddle River, NJ: Pearson and Prentice Hall.

Sandulli, F. D. & Chesbrough, H. (2009). 'Open business models: the two sides of open business models'. *Universia Business Review* 2: 12–39.

Schiemann, W. A. (2009). *Reinventing Talent Management*. Hoboken, NJ: John Wiley & Sons.

Schweyer, A. (2004). *Talent Management Systems*. Aurora, Ontario: John Wiley & Sons Canada.

Sears, D. (2003). *Successful Talent Strategies*. New York: Amacom.

Servitje, R. (2003). *Bimbo, estrategia de éxito empresarial*. México: Prentice Hall.

Skillings, P. (2008). *Escape from Corporate America*. New York: Ballantine Books.

Smedley, T. (2007). 'The powers that BAE'. *People Management* (November): 40–2. Available at <http://www.peoplemanagement.co.uk> (accessed June 4, 2010).

Smilansky, J. (2006). *Developing Executive Talent*. Chichester: Jossey-Bass.

Southwest Airlines (2008). *Southwest Airlines Company Annual Report 2008*. Dallas: Southwest Airlines.

Snow, C. C. & Snell, S. A. (1993). 'Staffing as strategy', in N. Schmitt, W. C. Borman, & Associates (eds.), *Personnel Selection in Organizations*, pp. 448–78. San Francisco, CA: Jossey-Bass.

Stahl, G., Bjorkman, I., Farndale, E., Morris. S., Paauwe, J., Stiles, P., Trevor, J., & Wright, P. (2007). 'Global talent management: how leading multinationals build and sustain their talent pipeline'. INSEAD Working Paper Series.

Stout, H. (2000). 'What happens when a small department outgrows its company?', *Wall Street Journal*, June 2.

Terjesen, S. & Viola Frey, R. (2008). 'Attracting and retaining Generation Y knowledge worker talent', in V. Vaiman & C. M. Vance (eds). *Smart Talent Management*, ch. 4. Cheltenham: Edward Elgar.

Thompson, A. (2004). 'And the rich shall live with the rich'. *Financial Times*, January 24.

Thorne, K. & Pellant, A. (2007). *The Essential Guide to Managing Talent*. London: Kogan Page.

Tower Perrin (2008). *Closing the Engagement Gap: A Road Map for Driving Superior Business Performance*. Tower Perrin Global Workforce Study 2007–2008.

Tulgan, B. (2002). *Winning the Talent Wars*. New York: W.W. Norton & Company.

van Eijnatten, F. & Putnik, G. D. (2004). 'Chaos, complexity, learning, organization: towards a chaordic enterprise'. *The Learning Organization* 11(6): 418–29.

Vance, C. M. (2008). *Smart Talent Management*. Cheltenham: Edward Elgar.

Vance, C. M. & Vaiman, V. (2008). 'Smart talent management: on the powerful amalgamation of talent management and knowledge management', in V. Vaiman & N. Van Dam, *25 Best Practices in Learning & Talent Development*. Northampton, MA: Lulu Publishers.

Volberda, H. (1999). *Building the Flexible Firm: How to Remain Competitive*. Oxford: Oxford University Press.

Webb, D. L. & Pettigrew, A. M. (1999). 'The temporal development of strategy: patterns in the UK insurance industry'. *Organization Science* 10(5): 601–21.

Wiersema, M. F. & Bantel, K. A. (1992). 'Top management team demography and corporate strategic change'. *Academy of Management Journal* 35(1): 91–121.

Wilk, S. L. & Capelli, P. (2003). 'Understanding the determinants of employer use of selection methods'. *Personnel Psychology* 56: 103–24.

Zuboff, S. (1988). *In the Age of the Smart Machine: The Future of Work and Power.* New York: Basic Books.

INTERVIEWS

This book was possible thanks to the support provided by a number of different firms. Special thanks are due to those who agreed to be interviewed as part of this project:

AGD: Adriana Urquía

AON: Ruth Robertson, Mariano Viale

British American Tobacco: Lai Heng Chin

Deloitte: Nick Van Dam

Dow: Sebastián Soria, Jennifer Pettinga, Usha Singareddy

elBulli: Ferran Adrià, Marc Cuspinera, Eduard Chatruc, Lluís Puick, Lluís García, Juli Soler, Pol Perelló, Oriol Castro, Mateu Casañas, Alejandro Digilio and Marisa Reig

Faena Hotel + Universe: Massimo Ianni, Maximiliano Broquen, Valeria Lois

Globant: Axel Abulafia, Federico Domínguez, Paula Vaquero, Guibert Englebienne

Grupo Bimbo: Martín Díaz Pavón

Lastminute.com: Rupert Stocker, Chrissie Wanless

L'Oréal: Alejandro Mascó, Francois de Wazieres, Jeff Skingsley, Emmanuel Joffre, Teresa Di Campello, Judith Ruiz De Esquide, Marie-Aude Torres Maguedano, Remi Lugagne, Anselmo Presencio, Natalia Gonzalez Valdez, Philipe Louvet, Deborah Fenwick, Alexis Rymarz, Alastair Rennison, Dorota Dziewska

Pfizer: Florencia Battilana

Puig: Eulalia Alfonso, Ester Córdoba

Royal Mail: Simon Haben, Louise Carthright

Syngenta: Bruno Frei, Waqas Hussain

INDEX OF COMPANIES

SUBJECT INDEX